UTICA BOILERMAKER

America's Premier 15K Road Race

JOHN PITARRESI
Observer-Dispatch

Foreword by BILL RODGERS

Edited by Jorge L. Hernandez
Observer-Dispatch

NORTH COUNTRY BOOKS
Utica, New York

UTICA BOILERMAKER

America's Premier 15K Road Race

ISBN 0-925168-89-0

Project editor: Jorge L. Hernandez, Observer-Dispatch
Photo editor: Mark E. Johnson, Observer-Dispatch
Photo researcher: Christian Fuchs
Fact checker: Frank Tomaino
Cover design: Ron Johns, Observer-Dispatch
Production: Sheila Orlin, North Country Books;
Audrey Sherman, Countryside Typography;
Nancy P. Best, Nancy Did It!

NORTH COUNTRY BOOKS
Publisher-Distributor
311 Turner Street
Utica, New York 13501
315-735-4877
ncbooks@usadatanet.net

Table of Contents

Foreword

The book you are holding tells of a dream that extends far beyond just a race.

Twenty-five years ago, I never could have imagined the impact the Utica Boilermaker Road Race would have on road racing and a community.

From the first race of 800 runners to its 11,000-plus participants this anniversary year, the Boilermaker has touched many lives—from the runners, their families and friends to the race organizers, volunteers, sponsors and the greater Utica community.

You should know that it is not just the 9.3-mile race that draws the fans—it is also the Youth Run, the 5K Run and—of course—the Walk.

This narrative tells of the years of hard work and the challenges involved in running, as in life—the Boilermaker tells the story of accomplishments and challenges that begin with lacing up a pair of shoes and setting foot on a course.

You, too, can be involved in the spirit of the Boilermaker as you join us in reliving years of memories and excitement.

Only then can you truly understand what it is about this race that makes it simply amazing, even after twenty-five years.

Earle C. Reed
Founder
Utica Boilermaker Road Race

Preface

There are some folks—I am among them—who don't think of running as just a sport, with athletes racing for the simple conclusion of reaching the finish line.

Running in races such as the Utica Boilermaker Road Race also gives athletes the opportunity to become part of a community event.

Tackling the 9.3 miles of hills and flats in Utica on a hot July Sunday makes every runner aware of the terrific corporate and civic support, and the thousands of citizen volunteers and spectators who all work together as a team with the same goal—to prove that the Boilermaker is among the very best races in the United States.

Runners can't help but be swept up by the energetic fever for the sport and the spirit of community found at the Health & Fitness Expo before the race, at the induction ceremony of the National Distance Running Hall of Fame, at curbsides with throngs of fans leading the cheers, at the post-race party and the awards ceremony at the F.X. Matt Brewery.

In creating the Boilermaker, organizers have made it the largest 15K road race in the United States, and the folks in Utica for twenty-five years have continued to show a generosity of spirit and goodwill that's not matched anywhere else.

When I first ran—and won—the race in 1983, I felt really good. I don't remember how I came to be invited to run that Boilermaker, but I do remember being treated very well before, during and after the race by everyone involved. That's a feeling that's been shared, no doubt, by the thousands who have run before and after me.

I am very psyched during this Boilermaker anniversary year because this race has become such a huge success. After the New York City Marathon, the Boilermaker is *the* race for New York State. And after almost twenty years of my continued participation in the Boilermaker, I still love coming back to Utica.

Let's never stop the celebration of life and sport that is the Utica Boilermaker Road Race.

Bill Rodgers
Summer 2002

Rodgers is a racing legend, the 1983 Boilermaker champion and four-time winner of both the Boston and New York City Marathons. He has been a fixture in the Boilermaker's masters division for the last decade.

Acknowledgments

Many people helped tremendously in the preparation of this book. The author alone, however, is responsible for any errors that mar the text.

Dave Oja of the Syracuse Chargers Track Club was especially helpful and made important contributions to rcsearch on the early history of the Boilermaker.

Others who are deserving of my gratitude are my editors, Jorge L. Hernandez, John Dye and Sheila Orlin; photo editor Mark E. Johnson; photo researcher Christian Fuchs; and the members of the *Observer-Dispatch* photo department—Angel Chevrestt, Mike Doherty, Nancy Ford and Beth Mundschenk.

Retired colleagues Les Diven and Frank Tomaino kept me on the straight and narrow with their proofreading and fact checking.

There are many others who made major contributions: Amy Hunt, Bob Ingalls, Joe Kelly, Gail Kislevitz, Dick Mattia, Don Mitchell, Earle Reed, Dave Reichert, Bill Rodgers, Phil Stewart, Kathrine Switzer and Joe Wilczynski.

The members of the *Observer-Dispatch* sports department, past and present—editor Craig Muder, assistant editor Jeff Wager, Aaron Christiana, Anne Delaney, Kyle Johnson, Laurent Lawrence, Ron Moshier, Tom Murray, Nick Sardina and Maggie Tomasek—deserve my sincere thanks for taking up the slack while I was on my own, away from the everyday grind.

My mother always wanted me to write a book. Easy for her to say. There is no formal dedication but, "Ma, this is for you."

John Pitarresi
Utica, N.Y.
Summer 2002

Introduction

There is something incredibly invigorating in recording how a community comes truly alive around a single event. The Boilermaker is that catalyst. It is far more than a race; it's a huge community celebration.

The *Observer-Dispatch* has been celebrating with the Boilermaker from the beginning, and each year our commitment to this wonderful event has grown. That commitment extends far beyond coverage of the race itself. Over the years, newspaper staffers have manned water stations, stuffed goody bags, organized entertainment, cheered from the sidelines and, of course, run.

On this 25th anniversary of this spectacular community party, we offer this book as a reminder of where it all began and how very far it has come. And we offer it in salute to the thousands of fine people, from the Mohawk Valley and far beyond, who have made the Boilermaker a truly spectacular, world-class event.

Donna Donovan
President and Publisher
The *Observer-Dispatch*

About the Author

Little did John Pitarresi know twenty-five years ago that a 9.3-mile run through the streets of Utica, N.Y., would rise to prominence as the nation's premier 15K road race. "No one really thought it was going to be a big deal," he says.

But things certainly have changed since 1978, when reporters assigned to cover the race came from the city desk of the *Observer-Dispatch* and not the sports department. By the race's third year, Pitarresi had changed his mind. "It was apparent that the Boilermaker had captured the public's imagination."

Pitarresi's stature as a reporter and writer grew just as the race's position in the world of distance running grew. While the race was in its formative years, Pitarresi developed his skills covering the area's minor league professional hockey and baseball teams and writing a weekly outdoors column. During those years, his understanding of the Boilermaker and road racing grew, too, and he has earned a reputation well beyond Upstate New York as a knowledgeable authority on the sport of running.

As the Boilermaker approached its 25th anniversary there was little doubt that the *Observer-Dispatch* would publish a book about the race, and there was no doubt that Pitarresi would be asked to take on this project. Beginning in January 2002 and continuing well after the race was run, the book would become a labor of love for John and many of us at the *O-D*.

"Although I thought I knew a lot about the race," he says, "I learned a lot more."

Two favorite races stand out in Pitarresi's memories of the Boilermaker: Bill Rodgers' 1983 victory in the men's division and Jill Hunter's 1991 win in the women's division.

"When Rodgers won the race in record time, he really lent a tremendous amount of credibility to the Boilermaker. He was the best known runner in the world," he says.

As for Hunter's unexpected win, "It was stunning because a lot of people had no idea who she was. She broke the record by a full two minutes and it lasted for ten years."

The race's reach has grown beyond the running world. "To me, it the biggest and best thing that happens in the Utica-Rome area each year. It's an opportunity for this area to put its best foot forward—to do something as well as any region in the country—and it does it," Pitarresi says. "I love this race." That is clearly demonstrated in "Utica Boilermaker: America's Premier 15K Road Race."

It's with a great sense of pride that we present this book to *Observer-Dispatch* readers, and to runners and running fans everywhere.

John Dye
Editor
The *Observer-Dispatch*
Summer 2002

John Pitarresi was born in Niagara Falls, N.Y., in 1948. A 1970 graduate of Hamilton College in Clinton, N.Y., he joined the *Observer-Dispatch* in 1973 as a sports writer after a two-year stint as a junior high school social studies teacher. He has covered the Boilermaker since 1984.

1978

The Germ of an Idea

1978 HIGHLIGHTS

MEN
Ric Rojas
USA, 45:38

WOMEN
Kathy Mills
USA, 54:26

MEN'S MASTERS
Kenneth Mueller
USA, 50:39

WOMEN'S MASTERS
Pat Bessell
USA, 1:05:04

Like all good things, the Utica Boilermaker Road Race started with an idea. Tom Hovey recalls that back in 1977 he and Joe Ficcaro—a longtime runner from Whitesboro, N.Y., a veteran of the Boston Marathon and a running guru who had shepherded a number of standout local athletes to college careers—had been talking awhile about putting on a race.

Others had informal discussions along the same lines.

Earle Reed was a sometime running partner of Hovey's and was looking for a way to celebrate the 50th anniversary of Utica Radiator Corporation, his father's company. A road race seemed like a natural to him.

It wouldn't be the first in the area, however.

The Utica YMCA Road Runners had established their Falling Leaves race in 1975—it's still going strong—and the Fort Stanwix Run from Rome, N.Y., to the Oriskany (N.Y.) Battlefield and back also had been run for a few years. The Utica Parkway Development Runs had started in 1970.

The Utica, N.Y., area already had a bit of running tradition, in any case.

Proctor, New Hartford and Notre Dame high schools had been producing outstanding distance runners for some time; Mohawk Valley Community College had a strong track and cross-country program; and there were several running clubs, including the Utica Pacemakers, the Roman Runners, the Steuben Striders and the Ferris Flyers—not to mention the Syracuse Chargers just 50 miles away.

So Reed gathered a committee of local runners, some with national connections, to put together a race. At the first committee meeting in September 1977 were Ficarro, Hovey, Jim McDade, Dave Pearce, Sam Gratch, Bob Carlson, Dick Mattia, Dave Reichert, Paul Ohlbaum, Randy Gates, Gerry Spaziani, Kevin Mahoney, Larry Lewicki and Fred Ferris.

The race quickly took form, and Hovey and Gates laid out the course, which started on Culver Avenue in East Utica near Utica Radiator, headed south onto the Memorial Parkway, up Valley View Road, onto Steele Hill Road and through the golf course, back onto the Parkway, west across Genesee Street onto Burrstone Road, north onto Champlin Avenue, east onto Whitesboro Street and then down Court Street to the finish in front of the West End Brewery.

The distance was set at 15 kilometers partly because that was the way it worked

Ric Rojas runs through a crowd at the finish line to win the men's division in the inaugural Utica Boilermaker Road Race. *Photo by Leo Hobaica*

out—Hovey's charge was to start the race near Utica Radiator and end it in front of the West End Brewery—and partly, Dave Reichert remembered, because it was close to 10 miles, a popular race distance at the time.

If the race needed any legitimacy and panache, Ficcaro and McDade provided it by securing Amateur Athletic Union sanctioning for the junior and masters divisions.

Reed asked his father, Utica Radiator president Robert Reed, and company treasurer Jim Benson for $750 to finance everything. He got it.

Twenty-five years later, the race budget is in the many hundreds of thousands of dollars.

"I didn't know where road running was going from there."

—Boilermaker founder Earle Reed, on the growth of the race

The first Utica Boilermaker Road Race was modest in size and scope, and gave little hint of what it would become.

There were about 930 entrants for that first run in Utica, on Sunday, July 16, 1978—and 782 finished. The winners—Ric Rojas and Kathy Mills, who were teammates on the national cross-country team—were the only competitors of national reputation.

No one could have guessed how things would change in twenty-five years.

The Boilermaker has evolved into a race of international stature, with 10,000 runners of every stripe—including the best road racers in the world—and has become the biggest and brightest athletic and social event in Central New York State's Mohawk Valley.

Rojas entered the race pretty much by chance—"serendipitous" is the term he used in describing how he found himself in Utica that day—and Mills, who had set the 5,000-meter world record earlier in the year, likely wouldn't have been here except that she lived in Fayetteville, N.Y., just forty miles up the road to the west.

While news of a new race sanctioned by the AAU was warmly greeted by area runners, it wasn't something that everyone in the Mohawk Valley immediately embraced.

The media coverage was minimal. The Utica newspapers, the *Daily Press* and the *Observer-Dispatch*, devoted less space to the event than they would to the heated Hamilton College-Utica College basketball rivalry of the time.

There were a couple of short advance stories and a hand-drawn map of the course. The day after the race, there was one story per paper, plus a few photographs. There was no list of top finishers, no first-person accounts, no related stories on interesting personalities. And if there was any coverage by local television and radio outlets, no one can remember it.

Even race founder Earle Reed, who didn't want to start "just another road race," couldn't imagine that the Boilermaker would evolve into a gargantuan undertaking that would require thousands of volunteers, give birth to a national Hall of Fame for distance runners and develop a beating heart of its own while enveloping the entire community.

Over its twenty-five-year history, the Boilermaker has become the nation's largest 15K road race, earned a place as one of the best-managed and best-loved events of its kind in America and stands as an enduring source of pride for the Utica-Rome-Herkimer County area in New York State.

It didn't start out that way, however. America's running boom was still in its early stages when the first Boilermaker was run. Frank Shorter had won the Olympic gold medal in the marathon in 1972 and added a silver in 1976, and Bill Rodgers was in the midst of his domination of the Boston and New York City Marathons. Running magazines were beginning to hit the newsstands, and writers such as Jim Fixx and George Sheehan were just starting to make names for themselves.

Distance running was still something of a cult sport. Before Shorter's Olympic victory, any American who ran much more than a mile at a time was considered a bit odd. There weren't hordes of people willing to pound out the Boilermaker distance of 9.3 miles, either.

Rojas, however, was one willing athlete; Mills another.

Rojas was one of the top runners in the country, a 1974 Harvard University graduate who had been a four-time state high school cross-country champion in New Mexico. A frequent training partner of Shorter's, he owned the top 20K time in America when he arrived in Utica, having entered the race almost by accident.

Rojas—who was twenty-six and living in Boulder, Colo.—had become friends with Lee Pollock, a Glens Falls, N.Y., native and former St. Lawrence University runner who had moved west several years before. The two were on a visit to Glens Falls when Rojas suggested they get into a race somewhere. There weren't that many around in those days, but Pollock had heard about the inaugural Boilermaker. The two came to Utica, met Reed and soon registered for the race.

Rojas and Mills—fresh from a great sophomore season at Penn State—were the only runners of note mentioned in the skimpy pre-race coverage in the Utica papers. Many top-flight local and regional high school and collegiate competitors also were registered, however—perhaps attracted by the fact the race was an AAU national championship.

In reality, though, few of the runners could keep up with Rojas or Mills.

Rojas finished in 45 minutes, 38 seconds, after taking the early lead and running away from everyone rather quickly, cruising the last 4 miles.

"I don't usually run that way," Rojas said after his victory, "but I felt comfortable today and decided I wouldn't wait until midway before I made my move. I knew I had a lead of about 300 yards halfway along, so I thought I'd just run a 5-minute pace from then on."

John Rayo, twenty-one, of East Syracuse, N.Y., was Rojas' closest competitor, and he was nearly 3 minutes behind.

Mills also had little trouble outdistancing her competition and referred to the run as just "a workout," but she won a national title in the 17-19 age group. A mark of how casually the race was regarded by the media is that her winning time is listed as 55 minutes in the *Daily Press's* account of the race. She actually ran 54:26.

A graduate of Fayetteville-Manlius (N.Y.) High School, Mills had won the national collegiate cross-country championship—then sanctioned by the Association of Intercollegiate Athletics for Women—in 1977, and set her 5,000 record (15:33:5) at the AIAW track championships at the University of Tennessee in the spring of 1978. Mills was a member of the Syracuse Chargers Track Club, a group that produced several other early Boilermaker champions—Tom Carter, Jim O'Connell, Ena Guevara-Mora and Mary Rybinski.

"I was training during the summer, and I wanted to put a hard effort in," said Mills, now Kathy Mills Parker living in Portland, Ore., with her husband and three children. Remembering the race, she

1978 Boilermaker women's winner Kathy Mills, left, races against Lynn Jennings in a collegiate meet in 1979. *Photo courtesy of Nancy Krueger*

said, "15K was a perfect distance. It was long enough to test you, but not long enough to kill you. And it was close to home. And they invited me."

As often was the case for women in the early days of road racing, Mills found herself surrounded by men and not really knowing any of her competitors. In fact, she usually didn't see them after the start. "You ran against yourself and the men," she said. "The only time I felt competitive was when I'd come up on a man."

Mills then would try to run down whoever it was, and usually did.

She went on to high finishes in national and international meets the next couple of years, but foot injuries began to take their toll, and she didn't race much after college. Mills still runs a couple of times a week, but spends more time on bikes and stairclimbers and lifting weights. She has pleasant memories of the Boilermaker.

"I just remember that it was a warm day, sunny," she said. "I remember thinking it was a pretty run through the neighborhoods. I thought it was a nice course. Actually, another thing. There was lot of community support. There were people who came out in their yards and put out their hoses for us."

That particular scene would be repeated and multiplied many times in succeeding years, and the community involvement and the crowds lining the course would grow to the point that runners from around the country ceaselessly marvel at the positive atmosphere.

Rojas and Mills dominated the race, but the home-grown talent didn't run badly. Bob LaSalle of Oriskany, N.Y., was ninth overall in 50:51, and Teri Tiso of Ilion, N.Y., ran 1:01:28 to win the women's open title, although that designation now is regarded as belonging to Mills, since she was the first woman overall.

Rojas would go on to win a number of big races, including Colorado's inaugural Bolder Boulder in 1979.

"I was really fit at the time," he said. "I was winning races by huge margins."

Rojas, the father of three, is a manager for a Boulder demolition company. He continues to compete, and also coaches runners through Ric Rojas Running and Running International. Rojas, who returned to the Boilermaker for the 25th race for the first time since 1982, when he finished fifth, is well aware of the reputation the event has earned over the last quarter century.

"Oh, yeah," he said. "The Utica Boilermaker is one of the top races in the country now. That's a great town and a great course."

Thousands of runners from across North America and quite a few from around the world seem to agree—now.

That first race made a mark, certainly, but no one really knew back in 1978 that it would light a road-running fire in the Mohawk Valley and someday bring the best distance runners in the world to Utica.

1979

Duel in the Sun

1979 HIGHLIGHTS

MEN
Tom Carter
USA, 47:15

WOMEN
Cindy Girard
USA, 57:30

MEN'S MASTERS
Brian Harris
USA, 50:58

WOMEN'S MASTERS
Barbara Backer
USA, 1:10:17

The heat was on when the second Utica Boilermaker Road Race was run on July 15. It was a sultry day—nearly 90° when the starting gun went off at 10:30 A.M.

The high temperatures might have played a role in the fact the victories of Tom Carter and Cindi Girard, both from the Binghamton, N.Y., area, were marred by the death of runner William Marceau.

Carter, a former star at Binghamton Seton Catholic High and then Niagara University and the University of Tennessee, vividly remembers the heat and his duel with favorite Don Howleson of St. Catharines, Ontario.

Carter was running well that year. He owned track records at SUNY Binghamton in the 3-mile (14:07) and 2-mile (8:55:5), and won the Rome, N.Y., Fort Stanwix Run later in the summer. He won the Boilermaker in 47:15, the slowest men's open winning time ever, but high temperatures had more than a little to do with that.

"I was running the race of my life, but it was so hot," said Carter, now the intramural director and cross-country and tennis coach at Broome Community College. "It turned into a survival run. Howleson was running 300 yards ahead of me. Just past the 8-mile mark, he started to slow down. I thought maybe, just maybe, I can do this. I ran 4:37 in the final mile and I caught him 300 yards down Whitesboro Street.

"I'll never forget going down that tunnel of people toward the finish line. It was like winning the Olympics," he said. "I'm a second-level runner. I'm not like a Bill Rodgers or the Kenyans. It's meant a lot to me. I'm grateful for the opportunity to win that race."

Carter is so grateful that he's back most years to run. "I love being a part of the event," he said. "I don't really run to be competitive anymore. Up until two years ago, I'd try to get in the top one hundred. Now I like to run it for fun. It's a victory lap."

Carter sometimes brings his basketball, which he spins at the end of a long pole to the delight of fans at the post-race party. Originally using a 16-foot, 6-inch maple sapling, he has worked his way up to poles nearly 40 feet long. He has performed his act more than 170 times at National Basketball Association, college and semipro games, earning up to $1,000 a night.

"That was my dream, going out and performing in front of thousands of people," he said.

A field of 1,228 runners registered for the race that year and 943 finished.

Marceau, fifty-nine, a science teacher at Westmoreland (N.Y.) High School, dropped to the pavement 30 yards short of the finish line. An experienced runner who had competed in the inaugural Boilermaker, Marceau was attended by finish-line worker Ralph Lupia and members of an auxiliary police medical team before being taken by ambulance to the then-St. Luke's Memorial Hospital Center.

Marceau's death and many complaints about the heat and humidity—thirteen runners were taken to area hospitals with symptoms of heat exhaustion—prompted race officials to move up the start of the Boilermaker to 9 A.M. in 1980. Carter, in fact, made that suggestion right after his victory. Race time was moved up to 8:30 A.M. in 1986 and finally 8 A.M. in 1994.

The Boilermaker also began to emphasize improved training methods and nutrition, plus safety precautions, to avoid similar tragedies.

"It turned into a survival run."

—Men's winner Tom Carter, commenting on the heat

"There was a significant amount of information put out in packets on proper hydration and other information disseminated before the race," said current assistant race director Dave Reichert. "We added a number of additional water stations and today [2002] there are twenty-four. We have the medical tent at the finish line, it's really a trauma unit, and there are several satellite facilities on the course."

While the death of a runner did mar the day, the Boilermaker had grown and attracted a more competitive field, although no one of the stature of 1978 winners Ric Rojas and Kathy Mills.

Carter outlasted Howleson, and Girard won the women's race in 57:30.

"It's so, so hot out there," Girard said after her win. "I liked the course even though I seem to run hilly courses even better. The race itself was great. There were plenty of water stops, and I hope to be back next year."

Cindi Girard of Binghamton, N.Y., won the women's division. *Photo courtesy of the* Binghamton Press & Sun Bulletin

Bob LaSalle of Oriskany, N.Y., and Terry Tiso of Ilion, N.Y., again were the top local finishers. LaSalle covered the course in 49:55 and Tiso in 1:02:29.

If the Boilermaker wasn't quite considered a very big deal yet, it was growing in importance and reputation. The runners certainly were paying attention.

"I think the Boilermaker might be the best race on the East Coast," said Jerry Smith of Syracuse, N.Y., in what was a typical comment of the time.

The spectators, growing in number, enjoyed it, too. "Terrific, marvelous," said Audrey Johns, one of thousands who watched. "I really enjoyed the race. I hope to see more like it in the future."

The Boilermaker also began to be noticed by local public officials and business leaders. In fact, Utica Mayor Stephen Pawlinga gave a short speech at the starting line and George Dastyck, publisher of the Utica newspapers, fired the starting gun.

"I couldn't believe the more than 1,000 runners at the starting line," Pawlinga said at the time. "This race brings a great honor to Utica. Earle Reed and his staff should be applauded."

Certainly, the Boilermaker name had spread in the year since its inaugural run.

Runners came from twenty-three states and Canada, although a large percentage of them were natives back in the Mohawk Valley on visits. And the media coverage, while not all-inclusive, had increased. In fact, the Utica newspapers published their first overhead photo of the race and also printed the names of everyone who registered in a special section devoted to what was termed then the Greater Utica Summer Festival.

The *Daily Press* published the first of many first-person columns by runners as City Editor George Newman related his adventures in battling his way to a far-back-of-the-pack finish.

The race was growing and after two years it already was a fixture on the local scene, although it was still far from what it would become.

Men's division champion Tom Carter celebrates after his victory. *Photo by Guy Danella*

Second-place men's finisher Terry Baker of Hagerstown, Md., runs toward the finish line in the 1980 race. Baker would return the next year and be second to none as he captured the overall title. *Photo by Leo Hobaica*

1980

The Taste of a Victory Beer

Fifteen years after she won the women's open title in the 1980 Boilermaker, Nancy Mieszczak had one extremely vivid recollection of that July 13.

"I remember never having a beer taste so good in my whole life," she said. "It was so hot."

Beer always has been a big part of the Boilermaker. After all, the West End Brewery, founded in 1888, now the F.X. Matt Brewery, was an original sponsor, and the race finishes right in front of the company's main office building.

The post-race party, which in 1980 took place in the brewery's visitors' parking lot (now it spreads out across the much larger parking lot behind the plant) is fueled by many gallons of Matt's products.

It was calculated that thirty-four half kegs of beer were consumed after the 1980 race, and 6,000 beer cups were used. The beer helped wash down about 2,500 hot dogs, too. That's an impressive level of consumption—except that those numbers would pale in comparison to later years.

By 1997, the brewery was donating 120 half kegs of beer for a party that drew thousands of runners, fans and family members.

Fred Matt, director of marketing for F.X. Matt, used close to 140 half kegs and poured about 28,000 twelve-ounce glasses of beer during the 25th anniversary post-race party in 2002.

Why would the brewery give away all that beer?

"One reason is that it is a premier event and any time you can attach your brand to a premier event, it's a good thing," Matt said. "We get local people and people from outside our area to drink our beer in a situation where they are hot and sweaty, which makes the beer taste even better than it normally does."

And a lot of people do drink the beer. More than 30,000 people now attend the post-race party, spilling out of the parking lot, over into Boilermaker Square across Hamilton Street and along Varick Street.

Mieszczak earned her beer in 1980, finishing in 55:02. Carrie Booth of Northampton, Mass., was second and Glenys Quick of New Zealand—who might have been the first overseas runner of any note to compete in the race—was third.

"I remember never having a beer taste so good in my whole life."

—Nancy Mieszczak, women's open winner

"I wanted to get close to 55 minutes," Mieszczak said after the race. "That was my goal. My strategy was not to kill myself going up the hills and to pick it up in the second half. It worked."

Peter Pfitzinger, twenty-two, a Cornell University graduate student, won the men's race in a record 45:16—21 seconds better than runner-up Terry Baker, a former Auburn University star from Hagerstown, Md.

"This is my first major road title," said Pfitzinger, who had finished third in Atlanta's Peachtree Road Race in Georgia on July 4. "I hadn't had a win until today."

Pfitzinger would go on to much more success. He won the 1984 U.S. Olympic Marathon trials and was eleventh and

1980 HIGHLIGHTS

MEN
Peter Pfitzinger
USA, 45:16

WOMEN
Nancy Mieszczak
USA, 55:02

MEN'S MASTERS
Calvin Loomis
USA, 52:05

WOMEN'S MASTERS
Becky Morris
USA, 1:09:27

WHEELCHAIR MEN
Marty Ball
USA, 53:30
(approx.)

Cornell University graduate Peter Pfitzinger completed the 9.3-mile race in 45:16 to win the men's division.
Photo by Leo Hobaica

fourteenth, respectively, in the 1984 and 1988 Olympic Marathons. He now lives in New Zealand, where he is an exercise physiologist and manager and lab director for UNISPORTS New Zealand. He writes the "Pfitzinger Lab Report" for *Running Times* magazine and has written several books, including *Road Racing for Serious Runners* and *Advanced Marathoning*, both with Scott Douglas.

Some of the 1,389 participants run toward the finish line of the 1980 race.
Photo by Leo Hobaica

Larry Frederick of Ilion, N.Y., was the top men's local finisher in 49:02, twenty-ninth overall. Carol Waters of Clinton, N.Y., led the local women in 57:09, fourth among the women.

Lou Roberts of Utica, N.Y., proved the race wasn't just for young legs. He was the oldest runner at seventy-six, and ran 1:38:42. The next year, Roberts actually lowered his time to 1:37:52 as he won his age category for the fourth straight time.

The 1980 Boilermaker also was distinguished by its first-ever wheelchair division. Inspired by other races that had established competition for athletes who use wheelchairs—there were about twenty such entrants in that year's Boston Marathon—the wheelchair division was a cooperative effort between the race and the Allied Resources Center for the Handicapped. Among the original entrants were Dennis English and Tom Mallabar of Utica; Jeff Koch of Middleville, N.Y.; and John Ferry of Oswego, N.Y.

The winner was Marty Ball, from Stanfordville, N.Y., who covered the course in about 53:30. "The roads, the crowd control, the traffic control—everything was superb," said Ball, who would win the Boilermaker several more times. "It was fine. I had a motorcycle policeman with me all the way."

In later years, the wheelchair division began to draw some of the top wheelchair racers in the nation. They included multiple Boilermaker winners Tony Nogueira, who won the New York City Marathon's first official wheelchair race in 2000; Jessica Galli; and Saul Mendoza, winner of a gold medal in the 1,500 meters in the 2000 Paralympics Games in Australia and the 2001 New York City Marathon champion.

Terry Tesak, who served for several years as the Boilermaker's wheelchair division coordinator, explained in 1999 that the committee's mission was to ensure that the wheelchair division continue to grow and attract some of the top names in the sport. Tesak said the committee also aimed to increase the public's awareness of wheelchair athletics and to show that wheelchair athletes should not be treated any differently from other race participants.

Michael and Nancy Mieszczak of Buffalo, N.Y., posed together after competing in 1980. Nancy won the women's division with a time of 55:02.
Photo by Leo Hobaica

Ball, now vice president of TI Sport LLC, a wheelchair manufacturer, calls the Boilermaker the top wheelchair race in New York, although he said he didn't feel totally welcome in the beginning.

Ball, who had polio as a child, had played wheelchair basketball since the age of nineteen, then was involved in sprint races for a while.

Those confined to wheelchairs were not thought capable of going long distances, he said, until Bob Hall's pioneering effort in the 1975 Boston Marathon when he raced in an everyday wheelchair. Ball competed in his first race at Falmouth, Mass., in 1977 and went on to race the New York Marathon unofficially five times. Ball turned sixty-five in 2002 and rolled his last long distance race in 2000.

The impact of wheelchair racing goes far beyond pure sport.

"Today the general public looks differently on those who use chairs," said Ball, who also credits running legend and 1983 Boilermaker champion Bill Rodgers with encouraging the development of wheelchair racing. "People who use chairs have become much more part of the mainstream. We've developed better [racing] equipment, so everyday wheelchairs have improved because of those innovations. People feel better about themselves; people are able to carry on more successful lives."

"There are so many things. We've found a lot more about using the upper body for mobility purposes. Chairs are now built differently to take better advantage of the upper body and not damage it. We've learned a lot about how to build a wheelchair, and how to train people properly to use one."

1981 women's winner Mary Rybinski, right, and 1980 women's winner Nancy Mieszczak, center, chat with Laura DeWald, who would return to capture the 1982 women's crown.
Photo by Leo Hobaica

More than 1,500 people competed in the fourth running of the Boilermaker.
Photo by Leo Hobaica

1981

Getting Even

Terry Baker got his revenge in the 1981 Boilermaker Road Race, Mary Rybinski lost her breakfast, and columnist Joe Kelly ran for the first time.

Baker, a former Auburn University star who still holds the school record in the 10,000 meters, had lost a very competitive race to Peter Pfitzinger in the 1980 Boilermaker.

The July 12, 1981, race—an Amateur Athletic Union national championship for 15K in nineteen age groups—was another duel between the two. Actually, Baker had already gotten even with Pfitzinger by beating him in Atlanta's Peachtree Road Race, just eight days before in Georgia.

This time Baker ran 44:48 on a hot, sunny day, breaking Pfitzinger's record time of 45:16. Pfitzinger came in under it, too, finishing in 45:08.

Rybinski, a relatively unknown Cortland State graduate from the Syracuse, N.Y., suburb of Minoa, ran 54:49 to win the women's open crown, outracing defending champion Nancy Mieszczak and Laura DeWald despite becoming sick halfway through the race.

Pfitzinger had pulled away from Baker late in the 1980 race. This time Baker made a strong move near Utica (N.Y.) College on Champlin Avenue and was in the clear by the time he hit the 8-mile mark just before turning onto Whitesboro Street.

"When we were going up that last hill, I said, 'He's not going to beat me where he did last year,'" Baker said after his victory. "So I surged and went for it about 100 yards from the top."

"He had it won at 7 [miles]," Pfitzinger said. "I had to get my retro rockets to catch him from there.

"It was a hell of a race. The heat bothered me early, but I felt good later. I ran better than last year, but Terry's tough. I figured it was going to be him or me this year."

The heat again played a major role, with another 9 A.M. start failing to ensure comfortable temperatures.

"On a good day I might have gone one minute faster," Baker said, "but it would have to be a better day than this."

Baker and Pfitzinger were known factors who entered the race as favorites. Rybinski was not. Still, she ran 54:49 to defeat Mieszczak (55:01) and DeWald (55:24). "I wasn't going to race too hard today, but I felt good at 6 miles and decided to go for it," Rybinski told reporters afterward.

What Rybinski didn't say at the time—and which was only revealed in 2002 by Syracuse (N.Y.) Chargers teammate and current president Dave Oja—was why she felt good at 6 miles. She felt lousy

1981 HIGHLIGHTS

MEN
Terry Baker
USA, 44:48

WOMEN
Mary Rybinski
USA, 54:49

MEN'S MASTERS
Ralph Zimmerman
USA, 48:51

WOMEN'S MASTERS
Pat Bessell
USA, 1:00:46

WHEELCHAIR MEN
Colin Dye
USA, 1:05:29

Ted Gurka of Endwell, N.Y., left, and Colin Dye of West Winfield, N.Y., get ready to start the race. Dye won the wheelchair division.
Photo by Leo Hobaica

Above: **Terry Baker of Hagerstown, Md., cools off after running to victory in 1981 with a then-record time of 44:48. Baker had finished second in the 1980 Boilermaker.** *Photo by Leo Hobaica*

Above right: **Volunteers line the route to hand out cups of water to thirsty runners.** *Photo by Leo Hobaica*

early in the morning, and when she crested the hill on the golf course, she thought she might throw up. A moment later, she did, right over her shoulder. But she never stopped running.

Rybinski certainly wasn't the first and absolutely not the last Boilermaker runner to leave his or her breakfast on the course, but most of the others didn't get the results she did. She passed Marian Testsch and then DeWald, and caught Mieszczak between 8 and 9 miles.

"[I] saw the opportunity to help something that I could foresee had such great possibilities."

—Joe Kelly, former O-D *columnist, on why he wrote often about the Boilermaker*

Mieszczak had taken the lead at 6 miles after thinking the other top runners would wear themselves out on the early hills, but hadn't counted on Rybinski.

"When she passed me, I knew it was hers," she said.

Larry Frederick of Ilion, N.Y., again was the top local men's finisher in 48:04, twenty-second overall, and Sarah Grygiel of New Hartford, N.Y., led the local women with a 56:40, one hundred ninety-third overall.

The race continued to grow. It was an AAU National Championship race again in all age groups, and ranked as one of the top seventy-five races in the country by *Runners World Magazine*. There were 1,550 entrants and 1,269 finishers, and many of them were outstanding local runners. In addition to Frederick and Grygiel they included Dave Brucker of the Utica Pacemakers (50:30) and Brian Fullem of the Ferris Flyers (50:48), along with Mike Kelly (54:07) of International Computers Limited, which had handled the race's timing since its birth.

The 1981 Boilermaker also was the first run by Joe Kelly, the Utica newspaper columnist who adopted the race and was closely identified with it for years. Kelly served on the Boilermaker committee and was the first director of the National Distance Running Hall of Fame. The many columns and stories he wrote went a long way toward popularizing the race in the Mohawk Valley. Kelly began writing his running column in 1983—an event he said changed his life—and devoted much of his space to the Boilermaker.

"I took advantage of the vehicle I had to promote something that was uniquely Utica," he said. "I had radio and TV shows, too, and saw the opportunity to help something that I could foresee had such great possibilities. I didn't want it to be just for runners. This is not just a race. It has to be marketed as a race of a world-class nature and as a community event."

Kelly's introduction to the Boilermaker came in 1980. He found himself stuck on Whitesboro Street, sitting on the hood of his car smoking a cigarette and biding his time as the runners in that year's race went by. He had never paid attention to the Boilermaker and had no idea the race was scheduled that day, but sometime during the wait he realized how much he was taken with the everyday runners who were trying to complete the course.

"Then I thought, 'I'd like to do that,'" he said. "I went on smoking, but I started to run. I eventually knew I had to run and lead that kind of lifestyle, or smoke and lead that kind of lifestyle. I elected to go without cigarettes."

The next year Kelly ran his first Boilermaker, then wrote a column about it. A couple of years later, he began writing the running column, and eventually ran races in nearly forty states.

Race director Earle Reed took notice and invited him to become part of his committee. For more than a decade, Kelly was assistant director, all the while beating the drum for what he believed was the best thing that ever happened to the Mohawk Valley. Kelly couldn't truly foresee what the Boilermaker would turn into, but even in 1981 it was steadily growing.

West End Brewery, Utica Radiator, the Utica *Daily Press* and *Observer-Dispatch* and International Computers Limited still were the major sponsors. There was a pre-race dinner at the Sons of Italy Lodge in Utica the night before, and the number of volunteers had grown to five hundred.

That number would multiply to more than 4,500 by the time of the 25th anniversary.

Mary Rybinski of Minoa, N.Y., glides toward the finish line on her way to victory in the women's division. Rybinski covered the 15K course in 54:49. *Photo by Leo Hobaica*

A racer enjoys a frosty beverage after the 1982 Utica Boilermaker Road Race.

1982

Running in Memoriam

Syracuse University senior James O'Connell had a couple of things going for him in the July 11, 1982, Boilermaker. History was one of them.

O'Connell already had a couple of Boilermaker titles under his belt. He won the 14-16 age group in the inaugural race in 1978 in 50:41 and captured the 17-19 championship in 1979 in 50:54.

He had some extra incentive in 1982. O'Connell ran the race wearing a black ribbon pinned to his jersey in memory of a friend who had drowned at Green Lakes State Park the week before. O'Connell, a member of the Syracuse (N.Y.) Chargers Track Club, had coached the young man, a member of the club's junior team. "I ran the race for him," O'Connell said.

The 1982 race was the first Boilermaker for Budd Coates, a former running star at nearby Camden (N.Y.) High School and Springfield College, and for many years now the health and fitness promotions manager at Rodale, Inc., publishers of *Runners World.*

Coates, still running competitively and a regular in the Boston Marathon, got into the Boilermaker pretty much because it was there, and to help out his brother-in-law. "It was a big local race," he said. "I ran the Fort Stanwix Race in Rome, N.Y., and that was originally the big ticket race in the area. But Utica, N.Y., kind of picked up and went crazy, and you'd have to come home and run it."

Also, Coates had talked his brother-in-law, Dave Gardner, into running and wanted to make sure he competed. "My hip was bugging me from slipping on the ice during the winter, but we had made a pact," he said.

Despite not feeling one hundred percent fit, Coates ran well, finishing fifteenth in 47:01. He did better in succeeding years, including a 45:38 in 1986 that was good for tenth place—the exact time Ric Rojas ran when he won the inaugural race in 1978—and 46:50 for seventh in 1987, on a day he recorded in his running journal as "hot, hazy, humid, yucky."

Like most of the outstanding local runners in the early Boilermakers, Coates' career began long before the race was conceived. He credited his high school physics teacher and cross-country coach, Vince Mellen, with getting him started.

"He took over a program that had two runners and by the time I was a senior we were league champions," said Coates, who had some outstanding teammates at Camden, including Jeff Milliman and Doug DeLaRoche.

The late Bill Coughlin, athletic director at Rome (N.Y.) Free Academy, had developed a Monday night running series at the Rome Fish Hatchery, along with his wife, Dee Howell Coughlin, and Bob Glover. That helped Coates, too.

"We'd have 5K runs and a gang from Syracuse would come down and a gang from Utica, and we'd battle them," he said.

Coates is still running hard—he ran the 2002 Boston Marathon in 2:28:49, seventh in the masters division—but is finding rewards other than winning or placing high. He said he was thrilled to be invited to the 2001 Ohme Hochi 30K road race in Japan to represent the Boston Athletic Association. He had raced in Ohme several years before and was highly regarded by the organizers.

As well as Coates was running in 1982, he couldn't get close to O'Connell, who ran very well on a day that began

1982 HIGHLIGHTS

MEN
James O'Connell
USA, 44:58

WOMEN
Laura DeWald
USA, 54:41

MEN'S MASTERS
Kirk Randall
USA, 49:44

WOMEN'S MASTERS
Setsu Rosen
USA, 1:07:50

WHEELCHAIR MEN
Marty Ball
USA
(time not available)

**Men's winner
James O'Connell**

**Women's winner
Laura DeWald**

Racers make their way through the crowd toward the finish line of the 1982 Utica Boilermaker Road Race. *Photo by Ed Miller*

cloudy and relatively cool before turning to sunshine.

O'Connell ran the 9.3 miles in 44:58, easily outdistancing a field that included three of the previous four men's open champions—Ric Rojas, Tom Carter and Terry Baker.

> *"Utica kind of picked up and went crazy."*
>
> *—Budd Coates, on why he decided to run his first Boilermaker*

Dan Predmore of Rochester, N.Y., was second in 45:34, with John Doub third in 45:49. Rojas was fifth in 46:10, Baker ninth in 46:26, and Carter sixty-seventh in 50:43. As usual, Ilion, N.Y.'s Larry Frederick was the top men's finisher from the Mohawk Valley, turning in a time of 47:58.

Runner Kathy Martin smiles as she's helped through the finish chute at Court Street.

Laura DeWald of the Washington Track Club and Arlington, Va.—who placed third in 1981—won the women's open race in a record 54:41. Nancy Mieszczak of Buffalo, N.Y., and the 1980 winner, was second in 44:45; defending champion Mary Rybinski was third in 56:09; and New Hartford, N.Y.'s Sarah Grygiel, the top local woman, was fourth in 57:36.

O'Connell dominated the race. He and Predmore had broken away from the pack by the time they reached Valley View Road, but O'Connell took off going downhill after the 4-mile mark on Steele Hill Road, and never was passed again.

Running alone at the head of the race, O'Connell said, wasn't all that comforting. He kept remembering a race in Cortland, N.Y., in which he was in fifth place with 300 yards to go and wound up finishing twentieth.

"I kept thinking, 'These guys are fast. Who's coming up?' Then I told myself to relax. I was watching the clock [on the pace-setting van]. I thought if I got past 30 minutes and was in the lead, I've got it."

Predmore found he had to back off

in the second half of the race after getting a stitch in his side, but was still pleased with the result. "I thought I ran a strong race," he said. "It's the first time I've raced against Jim since he's gotten good."

DeWald felt she earned some redemption for 1981, when she thought she should have won. She hadn't been able to train during the first half of 1982, and credited several weeks of intense weight training with giving her the victory. "With my [road] training last year, I felt I should have won," she said. "I've done a lot of weight training. I'm strong, but I'm not as fit. I had some trouble breathing. What I lacked in fitness I made up in strength."

Mieszczak, who finished in the top three for the third time in three Boilermaker appearances, said she knew DeWald would win after she broke away after 3 miles. "She pulled away from me and I just backed off," Mieszczak said. "I just backed off. I didn't say anything to her. I knew it was hers."

Mieszczak did, however, earn another silver bowl and, as she did the previous two years, she celebrated by enjoying a long drink of Matt's beer from it.

Wheelchair division winner Marty Ball, right, relaxes with an unidentified fellow racer after the race.
Photo by Dennis R. Floss

The race continued to grow. There were approximately 2,000 entrants and 1,572 finishers, but it would take an even bigger jump the next year, when road-racing superstar Bill Rodgers came to Utica for the first time.

Close to 1,600 runners finished the 1982 Boilermaker.
Photo by Dennis R. Floss

Renowned distance runner Bill Rodgers crosses the finish line with a record time of 44:38 to become the 1983 champion. *Photo by Darlene Drabick*

1983

Adding World Class

1983 HIGHLIGHTS

MEN
Bill Rodgers
USA, 44:38

WOMEN
Ena Guevara-Mora
USA, 53:22

MEN'S MASTERS
Ernest Dumas
USA, 50:10

WOMEN'S MASTERS
Betsy O'Neill
USA, 1:04:58

WHEELCHAIR MEN
Marty Ball
USA, 48:06

Through its first five years, the Boilermaker was a lot of fun. It had grown increasingly important locally, certainly. Nationally, though, it was just another race—until Bill Rodgers came along.

In 1983, Rodgers was—as he remains—one of the biggest names in road racing, although his great days as a marathoner were behind him. In fact, early that year, he won the last marathon of his career, in Miami, Fla.

Even at thirty-five, however, he was a potent force on the roads, and his decision to race in Utica, N.Y., that July 10 was seen as a huge boost for the race.

Boilermaker founder Earle Reed doesn't remember the details of bringing Rodgers here, nor does Rodgers. He just showed up, spoke at the spaghetti dinner Saturday night at the Sons of Italy Lodge, charmed everyone, went out the next morning to win easily in a record time of 44:38 and gave the race a tag that it has cherished ever since: "Bill Rodgers ran here!"

There had been any number of outstanding runners in the Boilermaker before Rodgers, but this was an athlete who shared with Olympic marathon hero Frank Shorter much of the credit for fueling the running boom of the 1970s.

"They are the Arnold Palmer and Jack Nicklaus of road racing," Reed has said more than once.

Rodgers had won the Boston and New York City Marathons four times each, with numerous other victories in important distance races, and had been the world's top-ranked marathoner three times in the 1970s.

Needless to say, having someone of his stature run the race was a major coup.

"It was an attempt to kick the race up a notch, that by having Bill Rodgers in we could bring the race to another level," said Dick Mattia, then and now the Boilermaker's coordinator of elite runners. "And it worked, obviously."

Rodgers' race in 1983 led to a jump in entries the next year, but there was more to it than that. "There was a significant change in recognition by the national media," Mattia said.

National running publications began paying attention to the race, and so did world-class runners. And if the public in the Mohawk Valley needed any more reason to get involved—the race already was a popular midsummer diversion for thousands of runners and non-runners—it was there.

"The thing about Bill was name recognition by the non-running population," Reed said. "He has a great personality. He's infectious with the crowd. They really like his spontaneous humor."

Runners set off at the start of the 1983 Utica Boilermaker Road Race.

Marty Ball of Rhinebeck, N.Y., won the wheelchair division with a time of 48:06. *Photo by Darlene Drabick*

Boilermaker announcer Phil Stewart, a former standout runner himself, publisher of the *Road Race Management Directory* and director of the Cherry Blossom 10K in Washington, D.C., invites Rodgers to his race each year and knows the value of the association.

"It was an attempt to kick the race up a notch."

—Dick Mattia, Boilermaker coordinator of elite runners, on Bill Rodgers' participation

"You have a combination of somebody who had great athletic performance and who is an incredibly personable guy," he said. "It's a great combination. When he was winning all those Bostons and New Yorks, that coincided with the first running boom. Millions of people were coming into the sport and watching. He was such an unassuming nice guy that he created this legacy."

Dave Oja, president of the Syracuse Chargers Track Club and a color commentator on Utica TV station WUTR's coverage of the race for many years, has a slightly different view of Rodgers' influence. He acknowledges that Rodgers helped to improve the Boilermaker's field and give it credibility to attract very top athletes, but feels that he has more influence now than he did then.

"Today, and for almost a decade now, Bill enjoys the status of a legend," he said. "Twenty years ago, he was enormously accomplished and talented, but not yet legendary. In addition, a larger percentage of the road-race fields today is impressed with celebrity. In 1983, a higher percentage of the other runners in the Boilermaker field wanted to beat Bill Rodgers rather than get his autograph."

Tom Smith of Utica, a former track star at Notre Dame High School in Utica and Providence College, ran the Boilermaker the first time that year, and turned in a time of 50:14, placing sixty-second overall. He had been in a race with Rodgers years before, but he said he ran the Boilermaker because Joe Ficcaro, his coach with the Utica Pacemakers, encouraged him to.

Smith had been running competitively since the late 1960s, before Rodgers was a star, and he would have run in 1983 whether Rodgers was there or not. "You'd always look up to a runner of that caliber. Bill Rodgers and Frank Shorter were guys whom you looked up to, but I was already motivated," said Smith, who didn't run the race again until a few years ago and is still turning in standout times for his age group. "But I'm sure Bill Rodgers coming to the race inspired a lot of people to run."

Most everyone associated with the Boilermaker feels Rodgers "made" the race. No doubt, organizers of many other races share the feeling. How does Rodgers feel about being regarded as such an important element in the building of the Boilermaker? He is typically low-key and self-effacing.

"It makes me feel really good," he said. "I came in there and was able to have a great race and was treated so well. They gave me those mugs [reproductions of the Schultz and Dooley beer steins that the F.X. Matt Brewery used to promote Utica Club beer for many years]. It had that kind of personal touch to it."

Rodgers said he liked the course, too. "It truly is a challenging course, and it's a great finish," he said. "It's kind of a little bit like a Boston. You've got to get through the hills and you've got the fans. I think one reason the Boilermaker is so satisfying is the crowds. You need them."

Rodgers still regrets that he was very ill the next year and unable to defend his title for one of the few times in his career.

He returned in 1989, however, when he ran fourth in the masters division in 47:32 despite a bad heel, and now he's back every year as a guest of Metropolitan Insurance and the National Distance Running Hall of Fame, which honored him as a charter inductee in 1998.

Rodgers is still running hard and is still very competitive. In fact, he was very put out after finishing second to Bob Giambalvo—54:12 to 54:20—in the 50-59

Runners snake their way through Utica during the 1983 race.
Photo by Ed Miller

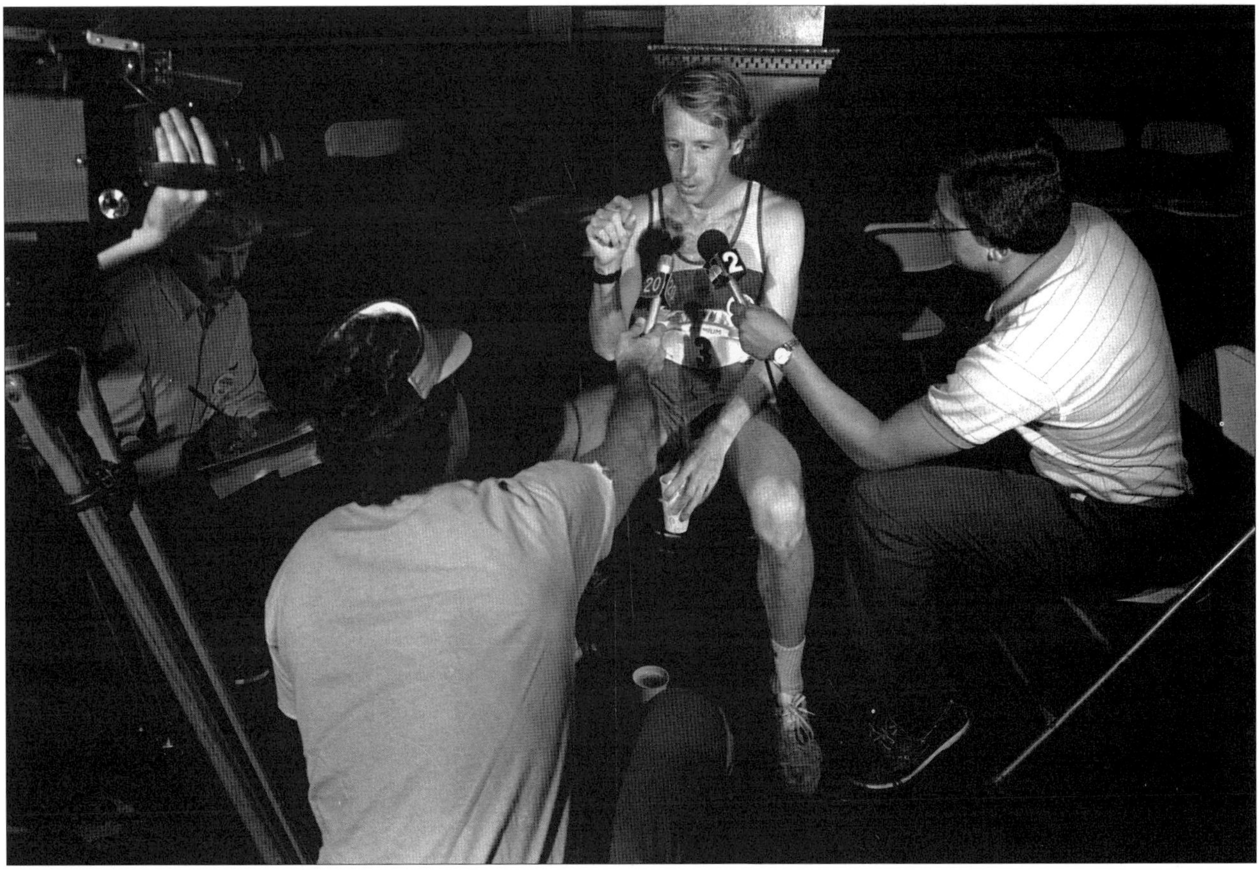

Running legend Bill Rodgers meets the press after his victory.
Photo by Darlene Drabick

age group in 2001. He was third in 2002, but faster—53:52.

"I am very psyched today because the Boilermaker has become such a great success, one of the key races in the country," he said. "To be a part of that, it's fun, pure fun, and I still come back because I love it and seeing everyone. It's the race for New York State, the biggest race except for the [New York City] Marathon."

The newspaper report of the 1983 race notes that Rodgers was happy to see that it was 65° and breezy for the 9 A.M. start. Although former champions Terry Baker and Jim O'Connell were in the field, the chief competition came from John Doub of Waynesboro, Pa.

Rodgers and Doub broke away from the pack on Valley View Road, and then Rodgers opened a 25-yard lead as they hit the Parkway after coming off Steele Hill Road. He looked back to see where Doub was.

"I do not have a great finishing kick, so I try to open as big a lead as possible when I can," Rodgers said after the race. "I believe you have to maximize your advantage as much as you can. At that point, I also knew there still was another hill to climb."

Rodgers worked up the long, gradual climb up Burrstone Road and then rolled downhill the last 2 miles to the finish as the crowd roared its approval. Doub was 41 seconds behind in 45:19.

Ena Guevara-Mora—a Peruvian marathoner and a member of the Syracuse Chargers who was living in Syracuse, N.Y., with her aunt—won the women's open race in 53:22, more than a minute better than Kathy Mills' 1978 record. She was far ahead of pre-race favorite Cynthia Lorenzoni, second in 53:58.

Guevara-Mora would go on to win again in 1984 and become the Boilermaker's first two-time open winner. "I believe a lot in the mental part of racing," she said afterward. "I try to compete within myself. I run at my own pace and forget about the other runners. When I'm out there, I feel like I'm a machine."

Ernest Dumas won the men's masters race in 50:10; Betsy O'Neill won the women's masters in 1:04:58; and Marty Ball again won the wheelchair race in 48:06.

Dave Brucker of Utica was the top local finisher in 47:58. The top local woman was Sheila Burth of Sauquoit, N.Y., who ran 1:01:45.

The exact number of entrants for the 1983 race has been lost, but it probably was about 2,400—at least five hundred more than the year before—and 2,134 finished. The Boilermaker continued to grow, and a letters column in the Utica newspapers reflected praise from around the state.

"One of the great success stories of the year," crowed Utica Mayor Stephen J. Pawlinga at the time.

That was thanks, at least in part, to Bill Rodgers.

Bill Rodgers, left, signs autographs for fans during festivities surrounding the 1983 race. *Photo by Darlene Drabick*

Ena Guevara-Mora of Syracuse, N.Y., stops her wrist timer as she crosses the finish line to claim the women's championship. Guevara-Mora won with a time of 53:22. *Photo by Darlene Drabick*

Runners begin to spread out shortly after the start of the 1984 race.

Young volunteers hand out cups of water to participants along the route.

1984

Women in the Spotlight

Bill Rodgers was unable to return to Utica, N.Y., in 1984 to defend his Boilermaker title, but the race did receive a visit from another road-racing pioneer, Kathrine Switzer.

Along with Rodgers, Switzer was invited to be the starter for the July 8, 1984, race by Joe Ficcaro, an old friend and longtime Mohawk Valley running guru. She would return to cover the race many times as a journalist and also to be honored as a member of the National Distance Running Hall of Fame's inaugural class in 1998.

"I fired the gun and then jumped into the race," Switzer remembered of 1984. She ran a very respectable 1:07:05.

The race was supposed to be a duel between Rodgers and Geoff Smith, but Rodgers couldn't compete because of an extremely bad cold. Instead, Smith and Ena Guevara-Mora, both of whom were about a month away from running in the Olympics in Los Angeles, scored relatively easy victories.

The Boilermaker also suffered through some controversy when confusion in the finish-line chutes led to incorrect or missing times and a good deal of griping by runners. That, in turn, led to some major changes in the race.

One unnamed race official suggested afterward that the time had come for a professional finish-line organization to take over from International Computers Limited, which had been timing the race since its first year. Race director Earle Reed didn't disagree.

"We definitely have to do something to make sure these problems with times don't occur in the future," he said.

By 1984 Switzer already had gained fame as the first woman to officially run the Boston Marathon, continuing to run after longtime unofficial director Jock Semple tried to rip her number off her chest and physically remove her from the 1967 race.

She also was the 1975 winner of the New York City Marathon, the originator and director of the Avon Running Program for women, and was well into a career as an award-winning journalist that began with a free-lancing trip to the tragic 1972 Olympics in Munich.

Switzer was no stranger to Central New York. She had earned bachelor's and master's degrees in journalism at Syracuse University, and had been coached by Arnie Briggs, an assistant track and cross-country coach at SU who had been a training partner of Ficcaro's.

"Arnie felt sorry for me because I was so slow," Switzer said. "He introduced me to long distance."

In the late 1960s, Switzer and Briggs helped organize the Syracuse (N.Y.) Track Club and held weekly 10K road races. "Joe Ficcaro always brought a group from Utica, and there would be a group from Rochester, N.Y.," Switzer said. "We'd run every Tuesday night."

Looking back, Switzer's appearance might have been most notable for the prescient statements she made in a post-race interview with Bruce Goldberg, then the sports editor of the Utica newspapers.

The first women's Olympic Marathon in 1984—which Switzer had helped organize and the advisability of which was still being debated in the sporting press—would be won by Joan Benoit in less than a month, with another long-distance legend, Grete Waitz, finishing second.

1984 HIGHLIGHTS

MEN
Geoff Smith
Great Britain, 44:21

WOMEN
Ena Guevara-Mora
USA, 52:36

MEN'S MASTERS
Kenny Inglis
Canada, 48:12

WOMEN'S MASTERS
Cindy Dalrymple
USA, 55:25

WHEELCHAIR MEN
Not available

Women's winner Ena Guevara-Mora

Runners and running fans mingle after the 1984 Utica Boilermaker Road Race. *Photo by Elizabeth A. Mundschenk*

"I think the future of the sport is extremely bright," Switzer said then. "Women's running hasn't even begun to peak. When we see on August 5 all these women in an event in which, seventeen years ago, an official tried to throw me out, we'll have a revolution in women's sports. Ten or twenty years from now, we'll experience tremendous parity in men's and women's sports and see great family participation in sports. We're going to push back the age limits."

"Women's running hasn't even begun to peak."

—Kathrine Switzer, on her first Boilermaker run

Eighteen years later, Switzer, who covers the Boilermaker each year for Utica's WIBX radio, had no reason to take back anything she said. "I think I was absolutely right. Look what's happened. In 1984, it was only one or two percent. Women now represent fifty percent of the runners in the United States. It's phenomenal. It has progressed in ways I never would have dreamed. It has nothing to do with acceptance. It has to do with accessibility and time. Women have adopted running as a lifestyle."

Age barriers already were being pushed aside back then, and have all but disappeared now. "What we have come to realize is that physical training for any age group increases strength," Switzer said. "The running population is getting older and older. People stay in the sport. The population of masters runners [forty and over] in the New York City Marathon is at fifty percent now. It's no longer just these old cranks or oddities who stick with it. Now it's everybody. It's a lifestyle. It's part of what they do."

Switzer did expect tremendous growth in the sport, especially among women, but she admits surprise at what the Boilermaker has grown into. "Who would ever imagine that it would become one of the most successful community events anywhere, when an entire town understands what's going on," she said.

But back in 1984, with Rodgers out of the race, Smith cruised to victory. In fact, he shattered the course record Rodgers set the year before, finishing in 44:21. He was pushed in the final 2 miles by Roland Davide (44:32) and Randy Thomas (44:39). Smith maintained a long lead most of the way, and his competitors had little doubt he would hang on to win.

"Randy and I gradually cut into his lead, but we knew even if we had caught up with him, he would have just turned on the jets," Davide said after the race. "This guy is an awfully hot runner. Even if Rodgers had been here today, he wouldn't have beaten him."

Actually, Rodgers had tabbed Smith the favorite just a couple of days before the race because he was a faster marathoner and in his prime, although he certainly didn't count himself out. At least, not until he became ill.

Smith, thirty, was the 1984 Boston Marathon champion, a former Providence College running star and British Olympian from Liverpool, England. He had led much of the 1983 New York Marathon before being overtaken by Rod Dixon in the last quarter mile. Still, he ran 2:09:08, the best time ever for a first-time marathoner.

A one-time firefighter and soccer player who didn't take up competitive running until he was twenty-two, Smith was training for the Olympic Marathon. He took the lead a little over a mile into the race, and really wasn't pressured after that. "I felt strong coming off the golf course," he said after the race. "I strained a groin, but I felt very strong. I didn't feel like I was killing myself. I just pushed a little bit."

Smith said he wanted to judge how his training was going for the Olympics—pretty good, obviously—and also break Rodgers' record by 10 or 15 seconds, which he did. The only problem he had was the weather. He was trying to prepare for the smog and heat of Southern California, and instead was greeted by blue skies and temperatures in the low 60s at race time in Utica.

Guevara-Mora became the first two-time champion of the Boilermaker by winning in 52:36, breaking the record of 53:22 she set in 1983. Former Herkimer County Community College in Herkimer, N.Y., instructor Teri Tiso, who had moved to Smithtown, Long Island, was second in 52:55.

Geoff Smith maintained a large lead for most of the 1984 race before winning with a time of 44:21. *Photo by Michelle Frankfurter*

Guevara-Mora was a member of Peru's Olympic Marathon team and had been training with coach Robert Yacono in nearby Norwich, N.Y., after spending the previous year running for Florida International University. Guevara-Mora and Yacono began training together the previous year, when Guevara-Mora was living in Syracuse, N.Y., and both were members of the Syracuse Chargers.

Kenny Inglis of Kincadine, Ontario, won the men's masters race in 48:12 and Cindy Dalrymple of Arlington, Va., won the women's masters in 55:25.

Dave Brucker of Utica, twenty, was the top local men's finisher again, in 47:36, eighteenth overall and 22 seconds better than his 1983 time. Ann Belfield of Waterville, N.Y., was the top local woman in 1:02:27.

The Boilermaker continued to build in popularity, and the number of entrants grew to 3,048—Rodgers' appearance the year before was credited by many with helping swell the field—with 2,510 finishers.

The numbers, however, might have begun to be a problem. There always had been a bit of talk among runners about the accuracy of times and the handling of the finish line, but the 1984 race brought out strong negative comments from some runners.

"The finish line, the chutes and the distribution of water was total chaos," wrote Tony Terzini of Utica in a letter to the Utica newspapers.

Terzini was one of several runners who expressed their displeasure, and many others complained publicly and privately. Some race officials blamed the problems on bandit runners, novice runners unfamiliar with the eight-chute finish-line system and uncooperative runners who clogged the chutes and argued with volunteers.

Race officials did promise changes, and they were made the next year.

Volunteers let runners know where they are on the 9.3-mile course on race day. *Photo by Elizabeth A. Mundschenk*

1985

A Credible Finish Line

The Boilermaker had a big problem as 1985 loomed, but the finish-line crisis got solved in a hurry, once race officials found the right people to take care of it.

The race that July 14, won by Irish Olympic marathoner Jerry Kiernan and Judi St. Hilaire, who broke the women's open record by more than 2 minutes, went off without a hitch. And the winners each earned $2,000 in the first Boilermaker to offer prize money, a growing trend in road racing.

The 1984 Boilermaker had not gone entirely smoothly, with problems at the finish line brought on by a steadily increasing field. Hundreds of runners were finishing close together, centered around the 72-minute mark, causing backups in the chutes and a good deal of confusion.

That led to a certain level of dissatisfaction as some runners found themselves without accurate times and places. Race director Earle Reed wanted that remedied.

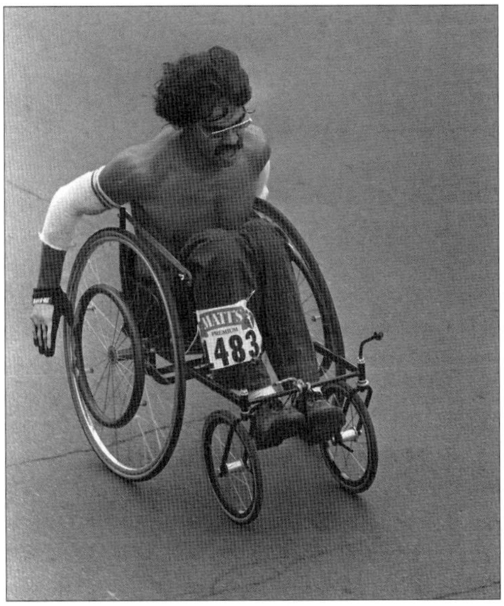

"Our attitude always has been, if we have a serious problem, we're going to address it," Reed said. "When I saw those runners looking at their watches, running in place, I knew we had to do something, especially if we wanted to grow the race."

Until 1985, the timing of the Boilermaker had been done by International Computers Limited, a local company that also was a major sponsor. Some officials felt the race, now with more than 3,100 runners, had outgrown ICL's capabilities.

"We came to a point where they couldn't handle it," said Dave Reichert, the Boilermaker's assistant director. "That finish-line chute configuration was changed probably four times [in the early years]."

The first couple of years it worked OK. After seven years, however, something was amiss. According to Reichert and Reed, ICL was ready to bow out in any case. "They just decided they didn't want to do it," Reed said.

The Boilermaker then called on people who spent a great deal of their time dealing with such things—Allan Steinfeld, then the executive vice president and technical director of the New York City Marathon, and Don Mitchell, a college professor from Buffalo whose company, Runtime Services, was becoming known as a top timer of big-time races around the country.

Steinfeld brought his expertise to Utica, N.Y., the day before the race, instructing the finish-line crew in the system he used in New York and going through a dress rehearsal.

"I told them, 'You might not believe this works, but it does,'" Steinfeld said. "It was simple. The race has such a fast

1985 HIGHLIGHTS

MEN
Jerry Kiernan
Ireland, 44:42

WOMEN
Judi St. Hilaire
USA, 50:35

MEN'S MASTERS
Ralph Zimmerman
USA, 51:05

WOMEN'S MASTERS
Cindy Dalrymple
USA, 59:02

WHEELCHAIR MEN
Jeff Koch
USA, 46:53

Men's winner Jerry Kiernan

Women's winner Judi St. Hilaire

Left: **Jeff Koch pushes his way to victory in the wheelchair division of the 1985 Boilermaker.**

Runners cross the finish line in the eighth running of the race.

finish because it is downhill, I told them to pay attention and do what you have to do. When it was over, they all looked at each other—they couldn't believe it. They didn't have the experience we had in New York. We had the opportunity to try different things in different races leading up to the marathon."

Utica Mayor Lou LaPolla takes the mike during the 1985 race.

Steinfeld's expertise made a huge difference in the quality of the finish, according to Reichert. "You're bringing in probably the best technical expert I've ever heard of," he said. "And he had a great group of volunteers at the finish line, all the resources he needed."

Steinfeld, now president of the New York Road Runners and director of the New York City Marathon, was glad to help out and glad to be working with good people. "This was a group that was excited by what they were doing," he said. "The Boilermaker takes over the city. It's a real positive thing, so you want to make sure everything goes well."

Providing for an orderly finish in 1985 was Steinfeld's job. Making sure runners got accurate times and places—and saw their names and places in the newspaper the next day—fell to Mitchell.

Mitchell had been timing races for a few years, and his biggest client was the Honolulu Marathon. He had been recommended to the Boilermaker by Dick Kendall, a veteran runner and The Athletics

Congress official from Buffalo, N.Y.

"There were about 3,000 runners at the time," said Mitchell, who teaches anthropology and archaeology at Buffalo State College. "It was easy. I don't really know what went wrong before. From the very beginning we didn't have any trouble. It used to be that these big computer companies would want to time races, and would say 'We can do this,' but they didn't really know how to do it. The little guy who is the specialist blows them away."

Mitchell now turns out the names of as many as 10,000 Boilermaker runners very quickly, with the time and place for everyone normally ready for printout by noon the day of the race. The Boilermaker's adoption of timing chips in 1999 has made his job much easier. He used to bring a staff of ten or twelve to assist in putting things together. Now, he doesn't need any help at all.

"It's still a pleasure to do the race," Mitchell said, "although it is somewhat different from the early days. It was a different feel then. It's more organized now. It's still the most exciting race I do. I have a 35,000-person 5K, which is extremely difficult, and that's fun, but there is no race that is as exciting as the Boilermaker with the elite runners and the way the community responds. I still can't get over the day city workers came and filled in a pothole near the finish line on Boilermaker Sunday."

"We came to a point where they couldn't handle it."

—Dave Reichert, now the Boilermaker's assistant director, on finish-line chutes

After straightening out the finish in 1985, Steinfeld turned the job over to David Katz, who still handles it through his Finish Line Road Race Technicians. Katz has worked two Olympics and is the veteran finish-line coordinator of the New York Marathon and the Millrose Games, but he still loves working the Boilermaker—and working with Mitchell, with whom he has partnered on many major races.

"One thing I've always loved about going to Utica is that the volunteers have been receptive and open-minded," he said. "They've always taken on the job with great pride. That's what makes the

Spectators cheer for George Zachary of Pittsville, Mass., from a porch on Court St. during the 1985 race. From left: Lula Eisnor, Zachary's mother-in-law; Barbara Powers and her son, Daniel; Zachary's sister-in-law Pat Servatius and her daughter, Amber; and Zachary's wife, Debbie.
Photo by Rick Bostick

A volunteer reacts when her cup runneth over as a runner grabs it during the race.
Photo by Rick Bostick

Boilermaker one of the greatest races in the country, because of the team effort. It's a great thing to see."

Katz's finish-line duties and those of the volunteers are simpler now in the days of computer-chip timing. The big thing is getting runners through the finish area and collecting the chips.

Timing wasn't of much concern to Jerry Kiernan, a thirty-two-year-old teacher, who had to deal with high humidity—not much of that in his native land—on a day that wasn't all that warm. The weather was oppressive enough to send at least four runners to the hospital and see another fifty treated at the medical tent. "You run for cover on a day like this in Ireland," Kiernan said after the race. "I was struggling like hell the last 4 miles. But pain is just fleeting. When you're out there, you put up with it. So I'll drink some beer tonight."

Medics rush a runner to the first-aid station during the race.

Kiernan, a strong uphill runner, took the lead from New Zealand's Rex Wilson at the top of Steele Hill Road and was never headed afterward. He finished in 44:42, with Ed Sheehan 17 seconds back, followed by Wilson (45:13) and defending champion Geoff Smith (45:24).

St. Hilaire, second at the Atlanta, Ga., Peachtree 10K on July 4, didn't seem to be bothered in the least by the weather or the injury she suffered in the 1984 New York City Marathon. She rolled to a record 50:35 finish, 2:01 better than Ena Guevara-Mora's 1984 record. Guevara-Mora was seventh, 4:23 behind St. Hilaire. "I was really pleased with the run," St. Hilaire said after the race. "I was scared of getting hurt again, especially on a hilly course, but I ran as hard as I could."

Michelle Annette Bush was second (52:25) and Jan Merrill third (52:47).

Jerry Lawson, the Chittenango, N.Y., native and Mohawk Valley Community College star who years later would set an American marathon record in Chicago, was the top local finisher (thirty-sixth, 49:34) in his first Boilermaker. Larry Frederick, of Columbia, S.C., formerly of Ilion, N.Y., was thirty-seventh in 49:44 and Jim Andrews of Hamilton, N.Y., forty-second in 50:20. Barbara Griggs of New York Mills, N.Y., was the top local woman (57:29).

Whitesboro, N.Y.'s Jeff Koch won the wheelchair race in 46:53. Ralph Zimmerman of North Tonawanda, N.Y., won the men's masters in 51:05, and Cindy Dalrymple of Arlington, Va., won the women's masters in 59:02.

The 1985 race also was marked by an adjustment of the course following new certification requirements mandated by The Athletics Congress. MVCC track and cross-country coach Dick Coleman and Wayne Nichols of the TAC measured and certified the course, which resulted in the starting line being pushed back 399 feet.

There were 3,134 runners registered and 2,624 finished, both records.

Rebecca Cramer of Wallkill, N.Y., gets a helping hand from nurse Cathie Boehlert after the long haul. *Photo by Tom Buchanan*

The lead pack of runners overtakes wheelchair competitor Thomas Nowhitney of Ballston Spa, N.Y., as they head up Culver Avenue shortly after the start in 1986. *Photo by Gary Fountain*

Runner Tim R. Reed of Clinton, N.Y., center, was among many thirsty athletes happy to accept a drink at the Coldwell Banker water station on the Parkway during the race. *Photo by Elizabeth A. Mundschenk*

1986

Running for Cash

It probably was the coolest Boilermaker yet, but it resulted in some hot times. It also was a good payday for Lisa Welch and Joseph Kipsang, who might have been running for free just a few years before.

Welch and Kipsang, who was the first in a long line of Kenyans to win in Utica, N.Y., both won on July 13 in record times. Welch ran 50:19, shaving 16 seconds off Judi St. Hilaire's record. Kipsang ran 44:07, breaking Jerry Kiernan's record by 35 seconds as he outkicked Jean-Pierre Ndayisenga over the last 200 yards, leading a parade of five runners who came in below the previous mark.

Cool weather helped the runners, as did the move to an 8:30 A.M. start time.

Welch and Kipsang earned some extra money, as the Boilermaker again paid $2,000 to the winners of the men's and women's open races, plus $500 bonuses for the record-breaking performances.

It was the second year the Boilermaker offered prize money. A $2,000 top prize might not sound like much today, but any money at all was welcome at the time, and not every race offered it. In fact, 1986 was the first year the granddaddy of all road races, the Boston Marathon, paid its winners. In 2002, Boston offered a total purse of $525,000.

Catherine Ndereba, the perennial Boilermaker and Boston winner, took home $363,500 in prize money in 2001 when she won fourteen of the sixteen races she entered, setting a record in the Boilermaker (48:06) and a world record in the Chicago Marathon (2:18:47).

It wasn't always that way. When Bill Rodgers came to Utica, in 1983, he won the silver bowl that was then given as a prize. The big payoff was the under-the-table appearance money he was paid, somewhere between $3,000 and $5,000.

Rodgers and other top running stars had been paid unofficially for many years because the governing bodies for track and road racing in the United States—the Amateur Athletic Union and then The Athletics Congress—would not allow them to accept cash payments. "You would talk to the race director and make a deal," Rodgers said of how he made arrangements for the Boilermaker and most other races in those days.

And they were good deals. In a 1983 story in *Sport* magazine, Rodgers hinted that his income from running and related business ventures was at least several hundred thousand dollars. Not bad for a guy who had to stay off toll roads when he drove to New York City for the first five-borough marathon in 1976 and then had to accept donations from friends to retrieve his car after it had been towed during his victory.

The Boilermaker had changed to a prize money format in 1985, for several reasons. "During that period of time, the races that have now become major events were all growing," said Dick Mattia, the Boilermaker's longtime coordinator of elite runners.

"There was competition among the road races, there was a continuous demand for appearance money. It was seen as something that could get out of hand, and the races could be controlled by the athletes. And it also put you in a bidding war with other races. If two races were very close together, you might have them trying to outbid each other, and you might have to pay an exorbitant amount

1986 HIGHLIGHTS

MEN
Joseph Kipsang
Kenya, 44:07

WOMEN
Lisa Welch
USA, 50:19

MEN'S MASTERS
Graham Tattersall
New Zealand, 48:50

WOMEN'S MASTERS
Diane Palmason
Canada, 1:01:33

WHEELCHAIR MEN
Bill McGovern
USA, 49:25

Women's winner Lisa Welch

Runners, including Jerry Kiernan, far left, of Dublin, Ireland, Jerry Lawson (37) of Utica, N.Y., and Steve Kogo (1407) of the Bronx, N.Y., sprint up Culver Avenue just after the start of the 1986 Utica Boilermaker Road Race. *Photo by Gary Fountain*

for athletes you wanted. It was not the best for the race or the general public," he said.

Mattia also pointed out another rarely mentioned factor in favor of prize money. "If you paid appearance money, there was no guarantee that the athlete would perform to his or her highest level," he said. "If someone did that, of course, it might hurt their appeal for the next year, and their longevity on the circuit."

The watershed event in the prize money movement—actually, in the movement for track and road-racing athletes to be openly financially compensated—was the 1981 Cascade Run Off in Portland, Ore.

Rodgers has referred to the race as a "trend-setter, a revolution," one that Gail Kislevitz thoroughly chronicled in the January-February 2002 edition of *Marathon & Beyond* magazine.

According to Kislevitz, a rebellion against the nineteenth-century English "amateur ideal" had been simmering for years as standout runners such as Rodgers, Don Kardong and others became increasingly irritated by running for laurel wreaths and bowls of stew—the prizes in Boston—plus under-the-table appearance money paid in greenbacks that everyone knew about but no one openly acknowledged.

The rules for amateurism for most of the last century were extremely strict. Not only could runners not accept cash prizes, they could not, according to the 1944 track and field handbook of the AAU that Kislevitz cited in her story, accept any prize worth more than $35. They could not sell or pawn a prize, knowingly compete with professionals or teach, train or coach for money.

By the 1950s, however, runners began accepting appearance money. The running boom of the 1970s encouraged athletic equipment companies to sponsor races, and there suddenly was plenty of cash available. Runners, however, could not openly accept cash because many of them were trying to secure positions on the 1980 U.S. Olympic team. That incentive ended with the U.S. boycott of the games that year.

Rodgers, Kardong, Greg Meyer, Joan Benoit, Lorraine Moller and others had formed the Association of Road Racing Athletes in 1979, with a goal of an open-racing system with prize money paid directly to runners.

Their rebellion reached a crescendo at the Cascade Run Off. Race director Chuck Galford got $50,000 in prize money from Nike, and he and the athletes defied the wishes of TAC head Ollan Cassell, who wanted separate finish lines for amateurs and pros and a list of declared professionals.

The athletes made their statement, and it was a powerful one. Eventually, the TAC worked out a deal with the International Amateur Athletic Federation and the International Olympic Committee to establish trust funds that athletes could draw upon for a variety of expenses. Even those restrictions soon faded away, and prize money in road races became the order of the day by the late 1980s.

Moller, who won the Boilermaker

Matthew Paul Bello watches the runners head up Culver Avenue through an upside down pair of binocluars as the race started. *Photo by Elizabeth A. Mundschenk*

masters title in 1995, was credited with one of the most quoted statements in road-racing history when asked how she felt after collecting her third-place winnings at Cascade. "It seems a little like losing your virginity," she said. "Maybe it has been something you cared about, but then it's gone and suddenly you sense there's a whole new world in front of you."

There remains to this day a disagreement as to what really changed the atmosphere. Most of the prominent runners of

Eventual winner Joseph Kipsang, left, begins to sprint past fellow runner Jean-Pierre Ndayisenga as the pair near the finish. *Photo by Gary Fountain*

the time felt they pushed the buttons.

Olympic gold medal winner Frank Shorter, an attorney, has maintained that it was the work that he and Cassell, also a lawyer and gold medal Olympian, did behind the scenes with the IAAF and IOC that led to the establishment of trust funds and the eventual acceptance of the open payment of prize money. In any case, the athletes began getting compensated directly, and the prizes have done nothing but increase ever since.

"There was competition among the road races."

—Dick Mattia, Boilermaker coordinator of elite runners, on awarding prize money

Welch and Kipsang certainly earned their money in the 1986 Boilermaker with great performances.

Welch's record came in her first 15K race and after she reached the starting area with no bib number. Race director Earle Reed dispatched Dick Markley, one of his employees at Utica Boilers, to her hotel to retrieve the number, and Welch was soon off and running. Her 50:19 erased St. Hilaire's 1985 record of 50:35. "I didn't think I'd get a record," Welch said after the race. "I was just thinking about winning and having fun."

Record times had been predicted because of the relatively cool temperatures. "That's probably the big factor in the time," Welch said. "I know when Judi St. Hilaire ran it last year, it was hot and humid. I'm glad it wasn't today. I was thinking, 'Don't be stupid and go out so hard like you always do.' I wanted to stay relaxed the first couple of miles."

Jan Ettle, who finished second, nearly 2 minutes behind, said Welch began pulling away a mile and a half into the race. She lost contact with her going through the golf course. After that, Welch just ran against the men.

Kipsang carved out his record time in a duel with Burundi's Ndayisenga over the last 2 miles, sprinting past his rival in the last 200 yards. "From the 9-mile mark, I studied him," Kipsang said. "I have a very powerful kick. I've never lost a race in a kick. He used up a lot of energy. He tried to drop me. Every time he turned his head to look back, he saw me."

Kipsang's win didn't quite give birth to a Kenyan dominance of the Boilermaker, but it did foreshadow what would happen a few years down the line. He would return and win in 1988 to become the race's first two-time men's open champion. In 1992, another Kenyan, Sammy Lelei, won the race, and Kenyans have won all but one of the men's open races since.

American runners, who already were having a tough time in distance races all over the map, fell further behind in 1986.

The only American in the top ten was Budd Coates, the former Camden (N.Y.) High School star who had moved to Emmaus, Pa. He was tenth in 45:38. Brian Fullem of Utica, a recent graduate of Bucknell University, was the top local finisher, in 47:48, twenty-fourth overall. Heidi Gerken of Vernon Center, N.Y., was the top local woman, in 57:30. Graham Tattersall won the men's masters race in 48:50, Diane Palmason won the women's masters in 1:01:33, and Bill McGovern won the wheelchair division in 49:25.

Bill Conney of Albany, N.Y., doesn't get a drink but does cool off with a cup shower as he bobbles the handoff at a water station during the race. *Photo by Elizabeth A. Mundschenk*

An undentified runner celebrates by leaping over the finish line at the end of the long run.
Photo by Elizabeth A. Mundschenk

Mark Roberts, left, races alongside Sam Ngatia during the 10th annual race. Roberts of Casa Grande, Ariz., went on to win the race with a time of 45:10. *Photo by Tom Buchanan*

1987

Steamy to the End

It was a classic scorcher of a race on July 12. England's Mark Roberts and New Zealand's Rex Wilson battled the heat, humidity, Sam Ngatia and each other in the 10th annual Boilermaker, with Roberts finally coming away with the victory in the closest finish to that point.

Roberts ran a 45:10, edging Wilson by 5 seconds. Becky Kirsininkas of Wheaton, Ill., won the women's race in 54:10, only 30 seconds ahead of two-time winner Ena Guevara-Mora.

All of them deserved medals for running on a day that was very hot and humid even for the traditionally steamy Boilermaker. It was in the 80s during the race—which again started at 8:30 A.M.—on the way to a high of 93° in mid-afternoon. The next day, temperatures hit a record high of 95°.

"We ran as tough as we could run," Wilson said afterward.

"There was no point in the race where I felt comfortable," Roberts said, referring both to the competition and the conditions. Roberts, though, was out there for 45 minutes. The majority of runners spent at least 70 minutes on the course, and a lot of them truly were uncomfortable. At least ten were treated and released at area hospitals, and one stayed overnight.

It was reported that many of the 3,060 entrants dropped out, but there were 2,597 finishers. That was eighty-five percent, pretty much about the average for all Boilermaker races.

One of the runners who finished and wasn't all that bothered by the weather was Fred Lebow, already a legend as the driving force behind the New York City Marathon. The colorful Lebow was making his first visit to the Boilermaker and said he really enjoyed himself.

In an interview with *Observer-Dispatch* running columnist Joe Kelly, Lebow ventured opinions on a few pertinent topics:

• On the Boilermaker itself: "This is a spectacle. This is great."

• On the Boilermaker spectators: "I was at Peachtree in Atlanta, Ga., and I think the crowds here are bigger, more enthusiastic."

• On the Boilermaker's downhill finish: "That's exactly the kind of finish I like."

• On what he wanted to do the night before the Boilermaker: "I wanted to go dancing."

• On Allan Steinfeld, his right-hand man then and his successor as boss of the marathon: "We are a good pair. He knows about computers and the stuff I don't know anything about. He is a genius."

• On Bob Bright, director of the Chicago Marathon, who had just changed the date of that race to reduce conflicts with New York: "We get along very well—now."

Lebow told Kelly he wanted to run the race in "1:09:59." He finished in 1:14:08. Considering the conditions, that was very, very good.

1987 HIGHLIGHTS

MEN
Mark Roberts
Great Britain, 45:10

WOMEN
Becky Kirsininkas
USA, 54:10

MEN'S MASTERS
Atlaw Beligne
USA, 50:26

WOMEN'S MASTERS
Bobbi Rothman
USA, 57:17

WHEELCHAIR MEN
Tom Nowhitney
USA, 59:00

Women's winner Becky Kirsininkas

> *"There was no point in the race where I felt comfortable."*
>
> *—Mark Roberts, men's open winner*

Lebow, a Romanian immigrant who would die of cancer in 1994, was hailed as a hero by everyone in long-distance running. He was inducted into the

A water spray offers a respite from the heat during the 15K race.
Photo by Elizabeth A. Mundschenk

National Distance Running Hall of Fame in a ceremony in Utica, N.Y.'s ornate Stanley Performing Arts Center in 2001.

"He loved the sport with a passion," the legendary Bill Rodgers said at the time, "and it showed. He ran sixty-eight marathons. He wasn't just a race director. He was one of our great spokesmen, the father of modern marathoning."

Hall of Famer Kathrine Switzer saw Lebow as a mentor and as a great popularizer of the sport, but more than anything, a believer in inclusiveness. "Fred was a champion of women, a champion of the underdog, really," she said. "He was a believer in including everyone. It wasn't all altruistic, though. He saw that women got publicity. He was the original win-win multi-tasker."

Boilermaker founder Earle Reed recalled that Steinfeld got Lebow to come to the Boilermaker. "He used to say he loved to go to races because he could steal some ideas," Reed said. "But it was an honor to have a guy like Fred Lebow come to Utica. We wanted to pick his brain, too. He basically took a small race and built it into one of the best marathons in the world."

Lebow's participation and his complimentary comments didn't hurt the Boilermaker one bit, of course. "It helped our credibility," Reed said. "It was like the Bill Rodgers' phenomenon. When Fred Lebow came, it was the same thing. He was very well-known not only among runners, but non-runners, too."

David Bauer, right, of Utica, N.Y., cools off a racer with a water shower after the run.
Photo by Gary Fountain

Roberts, Wilson and Ngatia weren't the biggest names in running, but they certainly put on a good show on a sweltering day.

Roberts, an asthmatic who went to Arizona to train and then ran for Central Arizona Junior College, Wilson and Ngatia broke away from the pack relatively early, heading up Valley View Road. They kept exchanging the lead along the Parkway and Burrstone Road before Ngatia, a Kenyan who ran for the University of Texas-El Paso, fell back at the turn onto Champlin Avenue.

"I kept checking those guys," Ngatia said. "I thought the race was in my hands, but it was not my day."

That left Roberts and Wilson to duel the last couple of miles. "I tried a couple of times between 8 and 9 miles to drop Mark," Wilson said after the race. "I couldn't. Then he couldn't drop me. We just tried to see who would fly down the hill."

They both did, but Roberts did it a little faster, grabbing the lead for good about a quarter mile from the finish.

Becky Kirsininkas set out to win her race, not set any records. Her time was nearly 4 minutes off the record set by Lisa Welch the year before, but that didn't bother her. "You couldn't push yourself too hard for a good time because of the conditions," she said afterward. "I tend to go out fast. If I went out at my usual pace in weather like this, I'd knock myself out at the 3-mile point. I tried to keep a comfortable pace the whole way."

Kirsininkas did not feel pressured by any female competitors. Guevara-Mora, who won the race in 1983 and 1984, got off a slow first mile, quickly losing contact with Kirsininkas. She did get her within sight late in the race, but there was no opportunity to make up the distance. "I wish it was a little longer," she said.

Atlaw Beligne, an Ethiopian who then was teaching at St. John's University, won the men's masters race in 50:26. Bobbi Rothman of Coconut Creek, Fla., won the women's masters race in 57:17.

Tom Nowhitney of Ballston Spa, N.Y., won the wheelchair race in 59:00.

Wheelchair racers Adam Deming, right, and Tom Nowhitney climb a hill. Nowhitney eventually won the race.
Photo by Elizabeth A. Mundschenk

Men's winner Joseph Kipsang warily checks on a running partner. The dog joined Kipsang for a few moments, and then returned to the sidelines of the 9.3-mile course. *Photo by Gary Fountain*

John S. Lisi, left, of Utica, N.Y., heads down Court Street toward the finish line in 1988 with his sons, Joey, 8, center, and John, 10. Joey was the youngest competitor in the race. His brother was the youngest in 1987. *Photo by Elizabeth A. Mundschenk*

1988

Minor Mishaps on Road to Victory

Joseph Kipsang enjoyed—perhaps the better word is endured—a colorful race on the way to winning the 1988 Boilermaker on July 10. Kipsang, who in 1986 became the first Kenyan to win the race, had to evade a careless spectator, dodge an errant automobile and outrun a dog to become the first two-time men's open winner.

Belgian Olympian Ria Van Landeghem rolled to the women's championship, and the race also received a visit from another icon of the ever-growing running community, Dr. George Sheehan.

Kipsang didn't create any of the color himself. He had it thrust upon him.

> *"I don't like dogs."*
>
> *—Joseph Kipsang, men's two-time open winner who had to outrun a dog*

Thousand of fans lined the course, as always, but the crowds were generally considered to be the largest ever at the Boilermaker.

A car somehow got onto the course at Burrstone Road, although it didn't really hinder Kipsang. Then a woman in the crowd at the intersection of Burrstone Road and Champlin Avenue, seeing the press truck drive by, stepped into the road to see where the runners were.

They were very close. She nearly collided with Kipsang before jumping back onto the curb. Farther down Champlin Avenue, a small dog ran at Kipsang, although it didn't appear to have any malicious intent. Kipsang didn't care. "I don't like dogs," he said.

Then, another automobile exited a cemetery on Champlin and camped on Kipsang's shoulder for a while.

Again, Kipsang wasn't bothered. Runner-up Mike O'Reilly wasn't happy, though. He complained about the dog and the cars, which he said the police should have done a better job of controlling.

Kipsang had to outkick Jean-Pierre Ndayisenga in a hot finish to set a record of 44:07 in his 1986 victory, a race that was run in extremely cool temperatures by Boilermaker standards. There were no dramatics this time around. The temperature was in the high 70s by race time, headed toward the 90s in the afternoon. A record fourteen official aid stations and many unofficial ones weren't going to make much difference.

"When I heard yesterday it was going to be 95°, I knew the record would not be within reach," Kipsang said. Fellow Kenyan Sam Ngatia helped Kipsang separate from the pack. The two of them led after the third mile, with local favorite Jerry Lawson and Brian Sheriff behind them and O'Reilly trailing. Kipsang dropped Ngatia going up Valley View

1988 HIGHLIGHTS

MEN
Joseph Kipsang
Kenya, 44:55

WOMEN
Ria Van Landeghem
Belgium, 52:45

MEN'S MASTERS
Bob Shlau
USA, 48:32

WOMEN'S MASTERS
Barb Filutze
USA, 57:05

WHEELCHAIR MEN
Bill McGovern
USA, 53:34

Dr. George Sheehan speaks to an audience of running enthusiasts at the Health & Fitness Expo the day before the 1988 Boilermaker.

Jerry L. Lawson of Chittenango, N.Y., drinks a cup of water, or most of one anyway, during the race.
Photo by Gary Fountain

Road. O'Reilly passed the others and began to make a move going up Steele Hill Road through the golf course.

"I'm a good hill runner," O'Reilly said. "I knew if I had any chance to beat him, I would have to catch him on the uphill." That didn't happen. Kipsang continued to build a lead, and eventually was one hundred yards ahead of O'Reilly. Neither the cars nor the dog derailed him.

Van Landeghem won the women's open in 52:45, with Debbie Raunig of Missoula, Mont., finishing second, 30 seconds behind. Again, the heat precluded any shot at a record, and Van Landeghem wasn't quite primed for one, anyway, after leading most of the way and then finishing second to superstar Grete Waitz in the Peachtree 10K in Atlanta, Ga., six days before. "I ran conservative because I ran fast last week," she said.

Raunig, who had run fourth in the 1986 Boilermaker and had the best American time in the marathon that year, was aware Van Landeghem was up ahead of her. "I was getting closer," she said. "I was drawing her in. I knew she was up there about 200 yards, but I was going to finish."

As a result, Raunig said she chose not to push. "It was more like surviving out there," she said. "It was hot. Hotter than Montana. I'm not used to the heat and humidity."

The heat apparently didn't bother Bob Schlau, who won the men's masters race in 48:32, a record by nearly 2 minutes. He earned the $1,000 top prize and a $500 bonus for a record. Atlaw Beligne, who had run a 50:26 to set the previous mark in 1987, finished second in 50:10. Barbara Filutze of Erie, Pa., won the women's masters in 57:05.

Bill McGovern of West Hoosick, N.Y., was the wheelchair winner in 53:34.

Bill McGovern approaches the finish line of the 1988 race. McGovern won the wheelchair division of the 9.3-mile course.

The race also was notable because it resulted in the best place (third) and time (45:34) ever for Jerry Lawson, the former Chittenango (N.Y.) High School and Mohawk Valley Community College running star.

Lawson, who still runs the Boilermaker most years, was nearly a decade away from his American record in the marathon. He ran under one of the unusual haircuts he became noted for—short and spiky on top with a pigtail down his back. "It's distinctive," he said. "It's easier to cool down."

Other runners with local connections did well, too. Budd Coates, formerly of Camden, N.Y., was eleventh in 47:31. Larry Frederick, formerly of Ilion, N.Y., ran a 50:16, and Lance Denning of Oneida, N.Y., ran 50:56. Heidi Gerken of Vernon Center, N.Y., was the top local woman with a time of 56:20 and Karen Vanderwood of Utica, N.Y., ran 1:03:03.

Sheehan's visit was the latest in a string of big credibility boosts for the Boilermaker. The first big jolt came when Bill Rodgers ran and set a record in 1983. Another came in 1987, when New York City Marathon director Fred Lebow ran the race.

Sheehan, a cardiologist, had been a standout college runner and then abandoned the sport for many years before starting in again at age forty-five in the early 1960s. His 1978 book *Running & Being* was a best-seller. That and subsequent books and his column in *Runner's World* magazine contributed to his reputation as the running game's foremost philosopher.

Sheehan conducted a running clinic the day before the race and also spoke at the Health & Fitness Expo, which took place in conjunction with the Boilermaker that year for the first time.

The big concern the day before the race was the heat, and Sheehan addressed that among many other issues in his Expo speech. "Don't worry about the ex-nun who goes by, or the guy with black socks," he told his audience. "The next time you see them, they'll be at an aid station. The story is the heat, not racing at all. I'm not sure anybody's going to die here tomorrow, but I think you should keep it in mind. You have to go out slow and slow down. You have to survive. That's going to be the badge: to survive."

After his talk, Sheehan privately discussed his two-year-old battle with prostate cancer—it would kill him five years later—and how it changed his life as much as running did.

Lured by pleasant associations provided by running, Sheehan had left his wife and twelve children several years before. After his cancer was diagnosed, he found he needed his family far more than he had imagined. "They have a saying about cancer," he said. "'Make every day count.' I'd been doing that, but what

Ria Van Landeghem was the top female runner, winning with a time of 52:45. *Photo by Gary Fountain*

I hadn't been doing was making every person count."

By the time he came to the 1988 Boilermaker, he obviously learned to do that. Sheehan did go out in the heat and ran the race in 1:18:41, a very good time on that day, especially for a sixty-nine-year-old, then declared the Boilermaker to be one of the top five races in America. *Runner's World* already had ranked it as one of the top road races in the nation earlier in the year.

Certainly, most everyone in the Mohawk Valley already thought so, and interest in the race never was higher. The crowds were large and enthusiastic, the volunteer participation massive and the atmosphere euphoric.

By this time, every media outlet in the area was fully involved in the race.

Utica's WIBX radio sports anchor Jim Jackson, who went on to an award-winning career as a radio and television broadcaster with the Philadelphia Flyers, provided continuous coverage of the race with commentary from Dick Mattia, a Boilermaker coordinator.

Other local radio stations—Rock 107 and WOUR—and television stations WKTV and WUTR covered the race from every angle in response to the enormous interest of the public.

SELLING FUN, RACE-RELATED GOODS

The Utica Boilermaker Road Race is more than just the race.

There are three golf tournaments associated with it. There is the annual Youth Run, the 5K Training Run, the 8K Walk—and the M&T Bank Health & Fitness Expo, which takes place for the two days prior to the Boilermaker on the grounds of the Masonic Home in Utica, N.Y.

"It's been a major success," said Bob McQueen, who has been chairman of the event for the last decade. "Our Expo is a lot different from the Boston Marathon's or New York City's. You go in there and people are selling things and it looks like Filene's basement. We have it on the grounds of the beautiful Masonic Home and everyone just enjoys the atmosphere."

As many as 25,000 might attend the Expo over two days, McQueen said, and there are between fifty and sixty exhibitors. The bulk of the booths are health- and sports-related. You can have your body fat measured or your blood pressure taken or even get a massage.

There is some selling at the Expo, especially of Boilermaker merchandise, food and sports drinks, but the emphasis is mostly on having fun and giving the exhibitors some exposure.

"We're not here to sell insurance," said Larry Gilroy of Gilroy, Kernan & Gilroy Insurance, a major Boilermaker sponsor. "We get to say hello to a lot of clients and a lot of old friends. The reason we're in the Expo and that we are a sponsor of the race is that we think the Boilermaker is one of the hottest things around the area and we are thrilled to support it in any way we can. It is a great morale builder for the whole area."

Gilroy, himself a Boilermaker runner—he ripped off an impressive 58:59 not long after he was out of college—loves the country-fair, family-oriented atmosphere of the Expo. Having the Youth Run there is a big plus, too.

"My kids always try to run the Youth Run, and that gives it a community, family feeling," he said. "That Youth Run has got to be one of the best things about the Boilermaker."

If you're a Boilermaker runner, you almost have to go, since the Expo is the site for packet and goody-bag pickup, and the Youth Run registration.

Bob Greene of Middletown, N.Y., who battled back from an automobile accident that crushed his legs, makes his way through the Yorkville (N.Y.) Fire Dept. water station on Champlin Avenue. He completed the race in about 2½ hours. *Photo by Elizabeth A. Mundschenk*

Linda Weibel-Kimmey of Clifton Park, N.Y., left, and her sister, Mary Janiszewski of Manlius, N.Y., approach the finish line of the 1989 Utica Boilermaker Road Race. *Photo by Gary Fountain*

1989

Race to the Finish

1989 HIGHLIGHTS

MEN
Jon Sinclair
USA, 44:06

WOMEN
Michelle Bush-Cuke
USA, 52:35

MEN'S MASTERS
Wilson Waigwa
Kenya, 46:09

WOMEN'S MASTERS
Ngaire Drake
New Zealand, 55:05

WHEELCHAIR MEN
Tom Nowhitney
USA, 1:03:16

Women's winner Michelle Bush-Cuke

The July 9, 1989, Boilermaker was notable for Jon Sinclair avenging an old loss to Bill Reifsnyder with a spectacular dash down Court Street to the finish, the return of Bill Rodgers and another strong performance by home-grown star Jerry Lawson.

Sinclair, from Fort Collins, Colo., thought he had won the Philadelphia Half Marathon back in 1985 with a strong finishing kick, but somehow Reifsnyder caught him at the tape and snatched his victory away. "Any time I see the guy, I think about that race," Sinclair said after the Boilermaker. "Now that won't be hanging over my head anymore."

This time, Sinclair's kick was good enough to beat Reifsnyder, but he had reason to thank his rival, too, for pushing him to a 44:06 clocking that broke Joseph Kipsang's 1986 course record by a second and earned him a $1,000 bonus.

Bill Rodgers was the road-racing legend who gave the Boilermaker a huge lift and an enormous dose of credibility when he ran for the first time in 1983, setting a record in the process. The 1989 race was his first time back, and he finished fourth in the masters division with a time of 47:32, far behind Wilson Waigwa of Kenya, who chopped more than 2 minutes off the masters record with a 46:09.

The ever-competitive Rodgers wasn't disappointed, because a heel injury had hampered his training for several months. "I tried to do my best, under the circumstances," he said afterward. "The next step is to become competitive with Wilson Waigwa and Victor Mora [who finished second]. Give me about another month, month and a half."

Sinclair, interestingly, was the first American man to win the Boilermaker since Rodgers. A couple of Englishmen (Geoff Smith, Mark Roberts), an Irishman (Jerry Kiernan) and a Kenyan (Kipsang, twice) had won the intervening five races as the United States' distance-running stock began to plummet.

Lawson ran well, finishing eighth in 45:41. That was a touch off his third place 45:34 of 1988, but the competition was getting tougher and, at twenty-three, he was still in the very early stages of a career that would see him become one of the nation's top marathoners, with the fastest times in America in 1993, 1996 and 1997.

Amazingly consistent in the Boilermaker, Lawson ran a 45:37 for ninth place in 1990, completing a four-year run of top ten finishes.

The 1984 graduate of nearby Chittenango (N.Y.) High School ran on powerful track and cross-country teams at Mohawk Valley Community College in Utica, N.Y., before going on to Boston University. He ran his first Boilermaker in 1985, placing thirty-sixth in 49:34. He's competed in all but three since.

"The Boilermaker has never been just another race."

—Central New York star Jerry Lawson on running again

Now, as one of the finest distance runners ever to be developed in Central New York—his 2:09:35 in the 1997 Chicago Marathon was for a time the American record in that race—he looks forward to returning to his roots each

Jerry Lawson, a 1984 graduate of Chittenango (N.Y.) High School, finished eighth with a time of 45:41. *Photo by Nancy L. Ford.*

Thomas Nowhitney of Ballston Spa, N.Y., rolls to another victory during the 1989 Boilermaker. *Photo by Elizabeth A. Mundschenk*

Gerry P. Seipp, left, of Buffalo, N.Y., and John T. Sullivan of Rochester, N.Y., cool off at a water station along the route. *Photo by Elizabeth A. Mundschenk*

summer. "The Boilermaker has never been just another race," Lawson said. "It's special because it gives me a chance to give back to the community where I started, to the people who supported me. You've got to take the time to give back."

Lawson remembers the 1988 race, his best finish, very well. "I was very pleased with that; I probably ran over my head," he said. "It wasn't even so much the time and place; it was having a local runner do that well."

Lawson didn't feel he could win—Joseph Kipsang broke the tape in 44:55, with Mike O'Reilley second in 45:18—but late in the race he knew he had a shot at a good performance. "At 10K, I realized I was fourth or fifth," he said. "I knew I wasn't that far out of it. I pulled up on Reifsnyder. I knew where 9 miles was and that it was downhill from there. As soon as we hit that, I started hammering."

He hammered all the way to that 45:34 finish, still the best Boilermaker time by a Central New York runner.

Lawson's running career began when a high school classmate encouraged him to go out for Chittenango, N.Y.'s indoor track team. "It wasn't until I got to the longer distances that I enjoyed it," he said.

He benefited from strong coaching at every level—Brian O'Keefe at Chittenango, Dick Coleman at MVCC and Bruce Lehane at Boston University. "I had great coaches all the way through," Lawson said. "Dick Coleman was a great coach, a great recruiter. The teams we had at MVCC during those years were phenomenal."

Lawson, who turned thirty-six just a couple of weeks before the 25th Boilermaker, feels he has plenty of running left. "I have something inside me telling me I haven't run my best yet," he said.

Then, there is always masters running, once Lawson hits age forty, but he has one major goal to hit before that—the 2004 Olympic Marathon. He was at the back of the pack in the 2000 Olympic trials in Pittsburgh—"That was a disaster," he said—but he is confident things will be different the next time around.

"I'm looking forward to that. There are only two guys who have run faster than me, and one only marginally, so I'm hoping maturity and experience will pay off."

In the 1989 race, Lawson and Reifsnyder had jumped out early. "I was going to push the entire way," Reifsnyder said afterward. Lawson, perhaps worn out after running Peachtree in Georgia a few days before, dropped back after about 2½ miles. Sinclair and Reifsnyder began to lose Rex Wilson going up Steele Hill Road and through the golf course.

Sinclair and Reifsnyder, nearly shoulder-to-shoulder, ran the 4th mile in 4:16. That was way too fast for Wilson, but he actually got back into the race and led briefly at the 6-mile mark near Utica College.

Wilson, however, knew that he couldn't win unless he opened a big lead because of the speed of his rivals. "The two guys I don't want to end a race with are Sinclair and Reifsnyder," he said.

Sinclair had figured it would come

Frank Domenico of Rome, N.Y., sprints ahead of James J. Bailey of Whitesboro, N.Y., during the race.
Photo by Gary Fountain

down to him and Reifsnyder, and he was right. His strategy over the last few miles was to sit behind his rival and wait. "I felt good out there, but I never felt good enough to drop him," Reifsnyder said. "I kept trying to drop him and that probably hurt me in the end."

Sinclair, knowing he had the ability to accelerate any time he wanted, waited until just after the 9-mile mark, then hit the gas and shot past Reifsnyder as the wildly enthusiastic crowd on Court Street screamed encouragement. "We hit that last light, and I sprinted as hard as I could," Sinclair said. "I just rolled downhill."

"He made the first move, and he just got away," Reifsnyder said. "He made a good strong move. It's a lot of fun running against Jon. Today he won, and he deserved it."

Jon Sinclair of Fort Collins, Colo., celebrates his victory just after crossing the finish line in record time. *Photo by Nancy L. Ford*

Michelle Bush-Cuke, who missed the 1988 race after getting married and getting out of shape, won the women's race in 52:35, edging 1980 Boston Marathon winner Jacqueline Gareau of Canada by 13 seconds in the second-closest women's Boilermaker to that point.

Finishing speed was the difference. "We ran together starting at mile 3," Bush-Cuke said. "She's experienced and a really good runner. I thought if I could stay with her, I could outkick her. But I wasn't sure."

Gareau figured she didn't have the speed to outkick Bush-Cuke and needed to get out early. She couldn't, and when they were still together approaching 8 miles, she knew she was in trouble. "She's going to kill me," she remembered thinking.

Bush-Cuke didn't do exactly that, but she did take off, and the race was hers.

Waigwa, who had just turned forty, shattered the Boilermaker's masters record, running 46:09, 2:23 faster than Bob Schlau had run the year before. Victor Mora was 17 seconds back, and Tony Simmons of England and Bill Rodgers also bettered Schlau's old record.

Ngaire Drake of New Zealand led a group of four women's masters runners who came in under Barb Filutze's 1988 record of 57:05, crossing the line in 55:05. Nancy Mieszczak, the 1980 women's open champion, was second in 56:05; followed by Claudia Ciavarella (56:30) and Nancy Oshier (56:47).

Drake said she could have run faster. "I expected to run in 53 minutes, so I had 3 or 4 minutes up my sleeve," said the playful Drake. "It would be silly to break the record by too much because I might want to come back next year and break it again. But you can't be too cheeky, because there might be someone who can beat you."

Tom Nowhitney of Ballston Spa, N.Y., was the wheelchair winner in 1:03:16. Mike Rinko was the top local men's runner (47:39). Karen Vanderwood was the top local woman (59:46).

1990

Local Runners Also Shine

No matter how large and prestigious the Boilermaker becomes, it never seems to outgrow the abilities of the standout runners who earn their spurs galloping over the hills and roads of the Mohawk Valley.

The Utica-Rome area in Central New York enjoyed a strong running tradition long before the Boilermaker was born, and local athletes jumped into the race with great enthusiasm when it was created in 1978. They've been dedicated to it ever since, and even top home-grown runners who have headed to other areas of the country come back nearly every year, no matter how far from home they have roamed.

"My friends and I always say it's great to be in Utica on Christmas, Thanksgiving and Boilermaker weekend," said Brian Fullem, a former Utica (N.Y.) Notre Dame High School and Bucknell University running star who now is a podiatrist in Connecticut. "I will always come back and run there, and I am thankful my parents still live 200 yards from the course, before the 3-mile marker."

Fullem ran his first Boilermaker in 1978 at age thirteen, and has rarely missed since. His best time was 47:48, good for twenty-fourth place in 1986.

Fullem was unable to run the July 8, 1990, Boilermaker, but other standout runners with Mohawk Valley connections—Jerry Lawson of Chittenango, N.Y., (45:37); Peter O'Brien of Herkimer, N.Y., (47:55); Patti Wiegand of Canastota, N.Y., (54:55); and Karen Vanderwood of Utica (56:34)—enjoyed great runs on a rather cool, low humidity day in the 60s that led to record performances.

Brazil's Delmir Dos Santos won the men's open race in a record 44:01, outdueling defending champion Jon Sinclair down the stretch.

New Zealand's John Campbell took

1990 HIGHLIGHTS

MEN
Delmir Dos Santos
Brazil, 44:01

WOMEN
Maria Trujillo
Mexico, 51:39

MEN'S MASTERS
John Campbell
New Zealand, 45:10

WOMEN'S MASTERS
Nancy Grayson
USA, 55:08

WHEELCHAIR MEN
Bill McGovern
USA, 48:50

Women's winner Maria Trujillo

Uticans Tanya Amodio, left, and her brother, Josh, give some of their neighbors encouragement near the finish line in 1990. *Photo by Elizabeth A. Mundschenk*

the men's masters race to a new level with a 45:10 clocking that was eighth overall and a world road race record for the 15K distance. Maria Trujillo of Mexico won the women's race easily in 51:39, and Nancy Grayson of Columbia, S.C., won the women's masters in 55:08, just 3 seconds off the mark Ngaire Drake set the year before.

"It's great to be in Utica on Christmas, Thanksgiving and Boilermaker weekend."

—Brian Fullem, Utica native who returns for the race

Those runners were introduced at the awards ceremony. The local runners, no matter how accomplished, occasionally are celebrated by the local media, but generally are known only to their friends and families and other members of the running community. Dozens and dozens of area runners have distinguished themselves in the Boilermaker over the years, and a few have even earned national reputations.

In addition to Lawson, O'Brien, Fullem, Wiegand and Vanderwood, a representative but not-all-inclusive list of top local Boilermaker runners would include Sarah Grygiel, Teri Tiso, Heidi Gerken, Nancy Frisillo, Christine Sisting, Susan Sivers-Corrigan, Gina Abraham, Mary Weibel, Barbara Griggs, Nicole Branck, Bob LaSalle, Budd Coates, Tom Smith, Larry Frederick, Jim Andrews, Mike Rinko, Dave Brucker, Ed Bruni, Marcus Gage, Chris Getman, Lance Denning, Steve Grygiel, Scott Humphrey, Mike Bronson, Jay Frisillo, Brian Dodge, Dave Jones, Dave Reichert and Dave Alteri.

Benny McIntosh—a 1985 graduate of Auburn (N.Y.) High School who starred at the University of Kentucky and would eventually run a sub-4-minute mile (3:58:25 in 1994)—turned in the best time ever by a Central New York runner, 44:45, good for fourth in 1989.

McIntosh, now a bank vice president in Lexington, Ky., still owns the New York state high school record at 10,000 meters (31:03) and is considering competing in the Olympic trials in 2004, according to his former high school coach,

Linda Weibel-Kimmey of Clifton Park, N.Y., reacts as she approaches the finish line. Nathan M. Hayes (1309) of Barneveld, N.Y., races nearby. *Photo by Elizabeth A. Mundschenk*

Al Wilson, who still coaches him.

Lawson, an All-American at Mohawk Valley Community College, has the best time of anyone with a strong Utica-Rome connection (45:34, third in 1988).

Coates, a Camden (N.Y.) High School graduate, ran 45:38 in 1986, believed to be the best time ever by a runner who grew up and competed in high school in the immediate Utica-Rome area.

Getman (47:18 in 2001) and O'Brien (47:20 in 1990) also had top times.

Gerken, whose family moved to Vernon Center, N.Y., while she was building an All-American career at Penn State, has the best time ever by a local woman, 52:50 in 1993.

Wiegand's best time was 53:35 in 1995. Sisting, of Marcy, N.Y., ran 54:24 in 1998, the hottest time ever by a woman who went to high school in the Mohawk Valley.

Whatever their times, though, the runners love the race and what it symbolizes. "The Boilermaker is part of the fabric of Utica and part of my running subconscious," Fullem said. "It is a race that is always in the back of my mind during training the whole year. I grew up running on the course. For me, running the race is like being home again as a seventeen-year-old with dreams of running the Olympics."

"I've run for a long, long time," said Smith, another former Utica Notre Dame star who went on to run at Providence College. "I really enjoy running in itself aside from racing. I think it's the best sport ever. It emphasizes the mental. You don't have to be big or tall [Smith is 5-feet, 4 inches and 130 pounds]. I think the Boilermaker really emphasizes that in this community. It really promotes the sport. A lot of people start running to run the Boilermaker, and some of them become hooked for life. Plus, it's a great party."

Gerken ran her first Boilermaker in 1985. The next year she ran 57:30 for eighth place behind Lisa Welch's record 50:19 and earned $50. "The reason I ran it the first time was just because it was there," Gerken recalled early in 2002. "Any race that ends at a brewery is OK in my book."

In 1990, eighty-four-year-old Charles Hackenheimer of Central Square, N.Y., heads down Whitesboro Street, on his way to finishing the Boilermaker in a time of 1:51:16. *Photo by Nancy L. Ford*

Yes, the beer tastes great after a long run, but there is more to it than that.

"If it's not the best, it's one of the very best road races I've run, and it has to be the best in the United States," she said. "Everything about the Boilermaker—I can't think of anything that is bad about it. The best thing is the folks

Delmir Dos Santos breaks the tape to win the 1990 Boilermaker in a then-record time of 44:01. "I think it's a great course, and you won't get better conditions anywhere in the world," he said after the race. "If you can't get a record today, you never will." *Photo by Elizabeth A. Mundschenk*

who are cheering, and they're cheering for everybody, not just those in front."

Not all the local runners who have run great Boilermaker times were high school or college standouts. There were no organized sports for girls when Nancy Frisillo was attending Utica Free Academy, and she didn't begin running until she started training for her first Boilermaker at age thirty-nine. "The reason I ran it is that I had watched previous years—all the enthusiasm and excitement—and it looked like a lot of fun," she said. "I decided to train for it. It probably was the most fun I ever had, an experience I'll never forget."

Frisillo, who ran other big races around the country—the Gasparilla Classic in Tampa, Fla., was one—ran her best Boilermaker in 1991, turning in a 1:00:52 to win the 45-49 age group.

Frisillo, who no longer races but watches the Boilermaker each year and celebrates the other runners, is modest about her achievements. "I put a lot of hard work into it," she said. "I always attributed it to the effort I put into my training. I don't think I had any natural ability. I think anyone who put the time and effort I did could do the same."

Frederick ran at Mohawk (N.Y.) High School and Albany (N.Y.) State and had been a top-flight racer for quite a while by the time the Boilermaker came around. He was third in the 1974 New York City Marathon, seventeenth in Boston in 1976. In 1981, he ran a 2:20:34 at Boston.

Now the owner of Run for Your Life, the largest specialty running store in Charlotte, N.C., Frederick said his running career got a major boost from Joe Ficcaro, the Boston Marathon veteran who had been supporting and encouraging Utica-area runners for many years. "I met him at a road race in Binghamton, N.Y." he said. "He gave me a Utica Pacemaker T-shirt. He always was really concerned about all the runners."

Frederick went on to be a 4:20-miler by the time he was a sophomore at Albany, but then he broke his leg, and his college career fell apart. Afterward, while working at Remington Arms in Ilion, N.Y., he

Marge Tuttle of Sauquoit, N.Y., plays some rock 'n' roll tunes as runners pass her on Court Street. "It peps them up," she said. Her son, Brent, of Whitesboro, N.Y., ran the race along with her niece and nephew. *Photo by Nancy L. Ford*

began training for marathons. He had to drive all over the East for races, so he was grateful to see a big event appear right in his backyard. And, like most everyone else, he still is grateful. His best time was 47:58 in 1982. In 2001, following knee surgery, he trotted along at a 9-minute pace, but he still loved it.

"The uniqueness of the brewery, the flyover by those jets, it was unbelievable," he said. "You've run 10 miles. You have a couple of beers. All is right with the world. The community involvement obviously makes the Boilermaker what it is. The chance they took in bringing in the elite runners, the community's grasp of it—I'm amazed. We have races in Charlotte, but the biggest race we have is 1,000 people. Everybody's involved here—everybody in Utica."

Runners Alice Root (3537) of Clinton, N.Y.; Stephen Frink (1053) of Mohawk, N.Y.; Steven Galinn (1077) of New Hartford, N.Y.; John W. Monroe Jr. (3492) of Utica, N.Y.; and Lawrence Yapeil (3243) of Ilion, N.Y., race toward the finish line. *Photo by Elizabeth A. Mundschenk*

The men's race in 1990 was a dramatic affair, with Dos Santos finally pulling away from Sinclair and Joaquin Pinheiro at the 9-mile mark. That trio ran together the last half of the race, with Pinheiro holding a short lead as they turned from Champlin Avenue onto Whitesboro Street. No one wanted to lead into the wind at that point, and the runners played a series of games trying to avoid that duty. Dos Santos snaked from one side of the road to the other for a while to try to get Sinclair to pass him.

After the race Sinclair said, "You want the other guy to do the work. We try to draft, like race cars do. It makes about an eight percent difference."

Bill McGovern of Hoosick Falls, N.Y., breaks the tape to win the wheelchair division of the 1990 race.
Photo by Elizabeth A. Mundschenk

Sinclair, who had beaten Reifsnyder in 1989 with a strong kick over the last quarter mile, tried to do the same against Dos Santos. He couldn't catch him, however, and the Brazilian took the victory.

Trujillo won the women's open race rather easily—1:27 minutes ahead of Angelica DeAlmeida who was second in 52:06—although she didn't think it was such a snap. She had finished third at Peachtree in Georgia just four days earlier and was just about out of gas. "I'll never do it again," she said after her victory. "Both races are tough races where I had to put in ninety to one hundred percent."

The taciturn Campbell, who also owned the world 10K road-race record at the time, was not mightily impressed with himself. "I don't try to go for records," he said. "But I'm glad I got a record. I'm glad it happened that way. I see guys running all over and chasing records for money, and I don't do that."

That said, Campbell did earn $1,000 for winning the masters division, plus $500 for the course record and $500 more the Boilermaker committee felt he deserved for the world record. Grayson, who became eligible for masters competition when she turned forty the previous April, would also win in 1991 and 1992. She finished well ahead of Claudia Ciavarella, second in 56:31.

Bill McGovern of Hoosick Falls, N.Y., won the wheelchair division in 48:50, with Colin Dye of West Winfield, N.Y., second. Nearly four hundred youngsters participated in the second annual Youth Run and Kathrine Switzer, the first woman to officially run the Boston Marathon, a track and field commentator for ABC and a Boilermaker competitor in 1984, called the race for Utica's WIBX radio from the media truck.

1991

Last American Champion

On July 14, 1991, Ed Eyestone became the last American to come in first. And Jill Hunter became the fastest woman to date to win.

Eyestone, a 1988 Olympic marathoner who would gain that distinction again in 1992, won the 1991 Boilermaker by outrunning Bill Reifsnyder and Steve Spence.

African runners—especially Kenyans—already were becoming major forces in the road-running world, but few could have foreseen that Eyestone would be the last American to win the Boilermaker. "I guess I hold the same title in a number of road races," said Eyestone, now the men's cross-country coach at his alma mater, Brigham Young University. "There certainly has been a great foreign influence that's continued to this day."

It was most predictable that Hunter's record run—her 48:19 clocking shattered Lisa Welch's Boilermaker 1986 mark by a full 2 minutes—would become a Boilermaker classic. The twenty-four-year-old Englishwoman, Reifsnyder's girlfriend at the time, didn't even decide to run until the morning of the race.

She then turned in a performance that was considered by some to be the Boilermaker's best ever—by man or woman—until Kenya's Catherine Ndereba, the queen of road racing at the turn of the 21st century, reeled off a 48:06 in 2001.

Eyestone earned ten All-American designations and four NCAA championships in his undergraduate days at BYU. In his senior year, he won the national cross-country championship in the fall

Kristen and Glenn Clark finish the race. *Photo by Elizabeth A. Mundschenk*

1991 HIGHLIGHTS

MEN
Ed Eyestone
USA, 44:10

WOMEN
Jill Hunter
Great Britain, 48:19

MEN'S MASTERS
Manuel Vera
Mexico, 45:57

WOMEN'S MASTERS
Nancy Grayson
USA, 55:15

WHEELCHAIR MEN
Colin Dye
USA, 44:04

WHEELCHAIR WOMEN
Connie Head
USA, 1:02:39

Men's winner
Ed Eyestone

Women's winner
Jill Hunter

Speeding toward the finish line is this unidentified runner in the 1991 Boilermaker. Photographer Elizabeth A. Mundschenk achieved the effect by using a slow shutter speed and panning the camera as the runner went by. *Photo by Elizabeth A. Mundschenk*

of 1984, then won the 5,000-meter and 10,000-meter championships back-to-back in the spring of 1985. He later hit the roads, and was the U.S. Road Racer of the Year five times.

By 1991, however, Latin Americans, Europeans and Africans were beginning to make their marks in American racing.

Bill Reifsnyder, who eventually finished second overall, leads the pack early in the race. *Photo by Nancy L. Ford*

That's what made the sight of Eyestone, Reifsnyder and Spence, shoulder-to-shoulder charging past the 9-mile mark of the Boilermaker, a memorable image—even now, more than a decade later.

"All three of us were running abreast for a while, which was nice," Eyestone said after the race. "Some people say American running is down."

Within a couple of years, many were sure of it. The Boilermaker certainly did its share to provide evidence. Kenya's Sammy Lelei would win the race in 1992, and no one but Kenyans and one Moroccan—world marathon record holder Khalid Khannouchi—has won since.

Eyestone thinks there are good reasons for that. For one thing, many of the best American runners are no longer running the roads, and many shy away from very competitive races like the Boilermaker. "You can go there and run a great time and not make a nickel," he said.

But Eyestone also acknowledges that there might not be as many Americans out there who want to work as hard as is necessary to be competitive in the twenty-first century. At the same time, he thinks there is some hope for the future. "Running is a hard sport, a hard vocation," he said. "You train your tail off to be one of the best. I think there is plenty of work ethic out there. I see new, talented kids coming up. I think the future is rosy. You're certainly never going to get the dominance that we had back in the 1970s and 1980s. Now the entire world is playing the

Connie Head of Binghamton, N.Y., wins the female wheelchair division of the 1991 Boilermaker. *Photo by Elizabeth A. Mundschenk*

game, but I still maintain we can have the occasional American who can run with the top people."

Eyestone, who won Atlanta's (Ga.) Peachtree 10K Road Race ten days before coming to Utica, N.Y., certainly could in his heyday. He outkicked Reifsnyder and Spence to earn his Boilermaker victory, finishing in 44:10, 3 seconds ahead of Reifsnyder.

Eyestone, who found time to coach his Cougar team to twelfth place in the NCAA cross-country championships in 2001 while also serving as columnist for *Runner's World* magazine and as television analyst for ESPN, remembers his victory in Utica well. "I remember it because it was a pretty important time for me," Eyestone said a few months before the 25th anniversary. "That one was crucial and gave me a great boost of confidence because the [U.S. Olympic Marathon] trials were coming up the next year. I wanted to be running my very best, particularly because I was facing some of the same guys I would in the trials. Reifsnyder and Spence were running very well. I felt very good winning because not only did I

Michael A. Sterling of West Winfield, N.Y., takes the semi-formal approach to running as he nears the finish line. *Photo by Elizabeth A. Mundschenk*

prove I could run with these guys, but also that I could put them down at the end. I remember Spence congratulated me and he made the comment that he wouldn't mind if the three of us finished that way in the trials."

It didn't turn out quite that way. The marathon trials were held in Columbus, Ohio, the next April, and Eyestone remembers Reifsnyder and Keith Brantly took off on Bob Kempainen, Spence and himself. "We were patient, though, and we caught them with 2 or 3 miles to go," he said.

Spence wound up winning, with Eyestone second and Kempainen third, and those three went to the Olympics in Barcelona.

The Boilermaker hiked its prize money in 1991, and Eyestone earned $3,000 for his victory. Hunter, who was one of the hottest distance runners in the world at the time, also got $3,000, plus a $1,000 bonus for her record. Not bad for someone who didn't decide to run until she got out of bed that morning. "I got up around five, had my tea and went out for a short jog," Hunter explained afterward in her north-of-England accent. "My legs felt OK, so at six I decided to run. I had a long run to do today, anyway."

Still, she didn't have any thought of going for a record. "I hadn't been feeling well," she said. "I was just going to run with the other girls."

That was not the case, however. The tiny but tough Hunter jumped ahead quickly and no one ever got close to her. Her 48:19 clocking was nearly 3 minutes ahead of Olga Markova, who had won the 1990 Marine Corps Marathon.

Favorable weather helped propel Hunter, too. "A perfect day to run—ideal conditions," Eyestone said afterward of weather that was reported as "cool, gray and humid."

The win was the latest in a long string of road-racing victories for Hunter. She had won the Gasparilla 15K and Washington, D.C., Cherry Blossom 10-mile race earlier in the year, among other events, and had just run the fifth-fastest 10K in history a couple of weeks before. If she didn't know for sure that she would have a record-breaking run, at least some of the competition did.

Lisa Welch Brady, who had run 50:19 in 1986, had little doubt. "When I saw her at the hotel last night, I knew my record was history," said Brady, who had returned to the Boilermaker for the first time since 1986, following her marriage and the birth of her first child. "Incredible. She's been incredible in every race she's run."

Brittany Powers has a good seat near the finish line of the 1991 Boilermaker on the shoulders of friend Dawn Dziegel, whose husband, Steve, ran the race. *Photo by Nancy L. Ford*

Eyestone remembered Hunter herself better than her run. "She was a popular runner on the circuit," he said. "She was a beautiful girl. For her to have that performance . . . and she might have been the first female runner of her caliber to come to Utica."

"Now the entire world is playing the game."

—Ed Eyestone, on becoming the last American winner to date

And the best for a very long time. Hunter's time was no longer the course record after the course was reconfigured in 1997, with four turns added because the starting line had to be moved up, but it remained the race record until Ndereba's 2001 dash. It wasn't even approached until then.

Manuel Vera of Mexico won the men's masters race in 45:57 and Nancy Grayson won the women's masters for the second straight year in 55:15. Colin Dye of West Winfield, N.Y., won the men's wheelchair race in 44:04, a course record, and Connie Head of Binghamton, N.Y., won the women's race in 1:02:39.

Pete O'Brien of Herkimer, N.Y., was the top local runner, finishing twenty-third overall in 47:20; Lance Denning of Oneida, N.Y., was thirty-ninth (48:52); and Mark Militello of Herkimer, forty-second (49:37). The top local women were Patti Weigand of Canastota, N.Y., twelfth (54:18); Heidi Gerken of Vernon Center, N.Y., seventeenth (55:47); and Karen Vanderwood of Utica, twenty-sixth (57:33).

The race continued to grow in popularity, both among the fans and the runners. There were 4,108 entrants from 36 states, three Canadian provinces and six foreign countries, and 3,636 finished.

It was the first time the Boilermaker attracted more than 4,000 runners, and the numbers were beginning to worry the race organizers, more because of the post-race crush than because of the number of entrants. "We don't want this to be just a mass of humanity," race director Earle Reed said.

The solution was to move the awards ceremony and post-race party to the large back parking lot at the F.X. Matt Brewery.

In 1992 a new era began, with five hundred more runners and, seemingly, many thousands more partygoers.

Colin Dye of West Winfield, N.Y., wins the wheelchair division in 1991.
Photo by Elizabeth A. Mundschenk

1992

Era of Kenyan Dominance

The July 12, 1992, Boilermaker was the start of something big. Actually, it was the start of a couple of things that were very big indeed.

Men's open winner Sammy Lelei's record-breaking victory ushered in an era of Kenyan dominance that hasn't ended yet.

Also, the post-race party took place in the large parking lot behind the F.X. Matt Brewery for the first time, allowing it to change into a huge, pulsating, high-energy affair that everyone seemed to love.

Favorable weather resulted in a number of race records. Lelei was red-hot coming into the race after winning the 15K Cascade Runoff in Portland, Ore., in June and then Atlanta's (Ga.) Peachtree Road Race on July 4. He just managed, however, to hold off countrymen Lameck Aguta and Godfrey Kiprotich on the way to a 43:39 clocking in the men's open race. The time chopped 22 seconds off the record Delmir Dos Santos set in 1990.

Although Lelei wasn't the first Kenyan to win the race, his victory was the precursor to the African nation's eventual dominance in road racing in general, and the Boilermaker in particular, for a long time to come.

Records also fell in the men's masters race—with Frenchman Pierre Levisse winning in 45:08—and the women's masters, with Nancy Grayson winning in 54:58 for her third consecutive title.

Madina Biktagirova of the Commonwealth of Independent States (the former U.S.S.R.), who won the Los Angeles Marathon in record time earlier in the year, was victorious in the women's open race in 50:22, well off the mark set by Jill Hunter the year before.

There also was a sad note in what had become the area's biggest day of fun when Ronald Tompkins of Marcy, N.Y., collapsed during the race and later died. It was the second race-related death in the history of the Boilermaker, the first since 1979.

The move to the brewery's back parking lot made it possible for many more runners and fans to enjoy themselves after the race. For the first fourteen years, the awards ceremony and post-race party

1992 HIGHLIGHTS

MEN
Sammy Lelei
Kenya, 43:39

WOMEN
Madina Biktagirova
Russia, 50:22

MEN'S MASTERS
Pierre Levisse
France, 45:08

WOMEN'S MASTERS
Nancy Grayson
USA, 54:58

WHEELCHAIR MEN
Marty Ball
USA, 45:06

WHEELCHAIR WOMEN
Connie Head
USA, 54:49

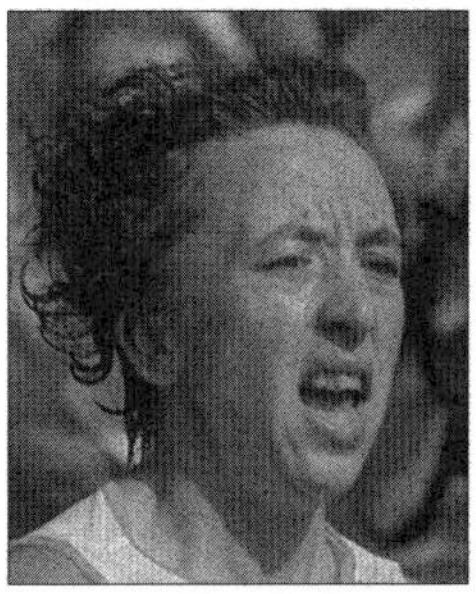

Women's winner Madina Biktagirova

Wheelchair racers sprint from the starting line. Marty Ball, second from right, would go on to win the wheelchair division.
Photo by Nancy L. Ford

took place in the small visitors' parking lot at the front of the brewery.

In 1991—when more than 4,000 runners were registered—runners, family members, friends, the media and anyone else interested found themselves crushed together and spilling over into the adjacent streets. "It was impossible," said longtime race official Dave Reichert.

An aerial view of the starting line of the 1992 Boilermaker.
Photo by Elizabeth A. Mundschenk

Race director Earle Reed had said after the 1991 race that another change probably would have to be made. "A survey of our runners told us that's what they disliked most about the race," Reed said of the crowding. "Now we can encourage them to hang around for the party and the awards ceremony."

And people certainly did hang around after the '92 race. Thousands of them drank, ate, danced, sang and listened to music. Their numbers seem to have grown every year since.

The race and the party grew together to the point that they are now inseparable. You don't have to run to go to the party, although it doesn't hurt. "It's like a 9-mile party," said Tom Smith, one of the top Utica, N.Y.-area runners in the race. "It really is nice."

And it really is nice because a lot of people work hard to make it that way. Tom Heiland, chairman of the post-race party committee since 1998, has about one hundred fifty volunteers who do everything in their power to make sure everyone has a good time.

"Everyone" is a lot of people. Heiland figures that between 25,000 and 28,000 packed the parking lot in 2001, and some 30,000 to 35,000 were accommodated for the 25th race.

The committee takes charge of innumerable details, including the annual flyover by F-16 fighters from the New York Air National Guard's 174th Fighter Wing, a brief but thrilling and powerful gesture that the crowd loves.

Also on Heiland's get-done list are the national anthem, water and ice-pop stands, the sound system, arranging with the brewery for beer, snow-cone machines, telephones, security, tables, chairs, baggage, plus cleanup by the Oneida County (N.Y.) Arc (an agency that provides services to developmentally disabled people)—and, of course, portable toilets, of which there were at least one hundred ten in 2002.

Heiland's involvement with the Boilermaker began in 1982 when his business, Utica Mack, offered to buy oranges to give to runners after the race. He soon had a crew that sliced thousands and thousands of oranges and picked up the peels afterward, but he wanted to do more.

Utica Mack still provides oranges, and Heiland goes out of his way to make sure everyone has a great time for several hours after the race. "We're very concerned about the runners' safety and well-being when they cross the finish line," he said. "We get them water, Popsicles, oranges. We want to make sure the runners are comfortable and secure after the race. And once they get to the party we have to make sure that everyone is responsible."

That last item has never been a problem, according to Reed. He can't remember any rowdiness, just a lot of good times.

"It is a great event, it has been a family event," Reed said. "Everyone knows it ends promptly at noontime. You do your awards in timely fashion, you get everybody something to eat, and then go home. The big reason we want to get people out by noon is that we've found that people have family reunions in the afternoon, and we encourage that."

Constraints on the post-race party might be the limiting factor in keeping the number of runners in the low five figures. The crowds already spill across Columbia Street and into Boilermaker Park across from the parking lot and back out Edward Street to Varick Street. There isn't much room left.

Lelei got to the party early after the 1992 race, as he and four others—countrymen Aguta, Kiprotich and James Kerri Kipyiko, and Alejandro Cruz of Mexico—all bettered Dos Santos' 1990 course record despite high humidity and bright sunshine. "It wasn't easy; it was very hard," Lelei said, after he and the other Kenyans dominated the race, taking nine of the top ten spots. A good showing overall, considering there were only ten Kenyans in the race.

Lelei, Kipyiko and Aguta set an extremely fast early pace, running together through a rapid 4:31 first mile. Lelei eventually pulled out to a 60-yard lead on Champlin Avenue, after 7 miles, but the race wasn't over.

Aguta and Kiprotich began creeping closer and closer, and then they chased Lelei wildly down Court Street the last several hundred yards, both finishing just a second behind in the race's closest finish ever. "I kicked too late," said Aguta, who ran for the first time in America.

"The hot pace right from the start was too fast for me," Kiprotich said. "I miscalculated. It was too late for me to catch up."

A volunteer offers a cup of water to a competitor along the race course.

The lead trio, including eventual winner Sammy Lelei of Kenya, far right, is cheered by members of the military. *Photo by Elizabeth A. Mundschenk*

Lelei was rewarded with a $5,000 prize—the purse had been increased considerably from the year before—plus a $1,000 record bonus.

"The hot pace from the start was too fast for me."

—Godfrey Kiprotich, on losing the race to a fellow Kenyan

Biktagirova, who would represent the Commonwealth of Independent States in the Olympics later in the summer, ran much of her race alone, but nearly was caught by countrywoman Albina Galliamova. Biktagirova finished in 50:22, with Galliamova just 6 seconds behind. "In the last mile, Albina almost got me, but I felt like I was going to win and I ran faster," Biktagirova said.

Biktagirova went on to finish fourth in the Olympic Marathon in Barcelona just a few weeks after her Boilermaker victory, but she was disqualified after testing positive for a banned stimulant, norephedrine, a drug that can be used to treat bronchial asthma.

Runners cross the finish line as the 1992 Utica Boilermaker Road Race winds down. *Photo by Nancy L. Ford*

Levisse and Grayson both had big days. Levisse killed two birds with one stone, avenging his loss to Joseph Nzau at Peachtree and setting a men's masters record of 45:08, 2 seconds better than New Zealand's John Campbell ran in 1990. "This was big revenge for me," said Levisse, who had set the 15K masters world record with a 44:14 at the Cascade Run Off a couple of weeks earlier.

Levisse was a bundle of Gallic charm after his victory, describing the win in colorful broken English and commenting on the large, enthusiastic crowds. "They were very friendly," he said. "They pushed me. They supported me."

And Levisse found inspiration along the way, especially from the cheerleaders he noticed as he crossed Genesee Street heading for the 6-mile mark. "The girls, I like," he said. "I look at them a few seconds. I am thinking, 'The race is not important.'"

Kiprotich liked the crowds, too. "I was amazed to see the course was packed," he said. "People were saying, 'Go, go.' The guys with guitars playing. I say, 'These guys must be crazy. They must like runners.' I am very surprised. This is a small city. I didn't know where all these people came from."

Grayson won her third consecutive Boilermaker, and finally got a record, breaking Ngaire Drake's mark by 7 seconds after coming very close the previous two years. "This year I was determined," she said. "I went off right from the very start at a pace that would get me that course record. It was a conscious move. In the past, I had gone out a little slower to make sure I had enough left. This year, I said, 'To heck with it.'"

Marty Ball, who won the first wheelchair title in 1980, won another in a battle with defending champion Colin Dye of West Winfield, N.Y., finishing in 45:06 to Dye's 45:51.

In its 15th year, the race continued to be a great and growing success, but the

Sammy Lelei of Kenya wins the men's division with a time of 43:39.

death of Tompkins, fifty-four, added a sad note. Tompkins had suffered from heart problems, but had entered every Boilermaker since 1982. He collapsed onto the shoulder of Champlin Avenue just short of the 7-mile mark and was declared dead of a heart attack an hour later at St. Elizabeth's hospital.

A team of nurses and doctors tried to aid Tompkins, but could not revive him.

Robert Wineburg of Greensboro, N.C., still has energy for a smile and a wave as he nears the end of the 15K race. *Photo by Elizabeth A. Mundschenk*

Dr. Sharon Mace, emergency room director at St. Elizabeth's, said Tompkins had a defective heart valve that made him susceptible to irregular heartbeats.

Among those who tried to revive him were doctors William Hall of Whitesboro, N.Y., and Nathan Keever of Hamilton, N.Y., both of whom had been running the race. They climbed into the ambulance that took Tompkins to St. Elizabeth's and assisted Dr. Mace in her efforts, then returned to the spot on Champlin Avenue where they had stopped to help the stricken runner. Hall and Keever began running again, although the race officially was over.

In a demonstration of the kind of spirit the Boilermaker generates, however, bystanders began applauding, a disc jockey cranked up the music and one water station stayed in business with just a couple of additional cups. A little more than two miles later, Hall and Keever finished the race side-by-side.

Linda Fatata of Utica, N.Y., who came in dead last, gets a kiss from Patricia Scaramella after completing the race on Sunday, July 14, 2002. "I'm dying, I'm dying," Fatata said. "I am walking but I am dying. I really didn't think I was going to finish, but I did." *Photo by Nancy L. Ford*

Mary E. Noga of Forestport, N.Y., raises her arms as she runs through a spray of water on Court Street during the race. *Photo by Nancy L. Ford*

Saul Mendoza of Snellville, Ga., heads up Valley View Road. He won the wheelchair division of the 2001 Boilermaker. Mendoza also won the 2000 race.
Photo by Elizabeth A. Mundschenk

Luane Davis gets a hug from her fiancé, Peter Haggerty, after she completed her first Boilermaker in 2000. The couple, both from Rochester, N.Y., ran together. *Photo by Elizabeth A. Mundschenk*

The lead runners in the men's division make their way through Valley View Golf Course during the 25th Boilermaker in 2002. *Photo by Mark E. Johnson*

Participants jump off at the starting line of the 1985 Boilermaker.

Ann Moracco of Clinton, N.Y., hands out water to runners along the Memorial Parkway during the 1994 race. *Photo by Elizabeth A. Mundschenk*

Young fans prepare to exchange a high-five during the 1994 Boilermaker. *Photo by Elizabeth A. Mundschenk*

Laurie J. Stephens of Wenham, Mass., makes her way through the Valley View Golf Course in the 2001 race. *Photo by Elizabeth A. Mundschenk*

Carl Aiken, center, of East Greenbush, N.Y., squeezes past Inge Aiken, also of East Greenbush, left, and an unidentified runner at the finish line of the 25th Boilermaker in 2002. *Photo by Elizabeth A. Mundschenk*

The leader pack makes its way up Valley View Road in the 25th Boilermaker Road Race in Utica on Sunday, July 14, 2002. *Photo by Elizabeth A. Mundschenk*

The Culver Avenue ramp over Route 5 is crowded with runners awaiting the starter's gun in 1992. *Photo by Elizabeth A. Mundschenk*

With cameras in hand, Sue Ball of Herkimer, N.Y., left, and Tina and Charlie Sarris of Schenectedy, N.Y., watch out for family members on Court Street during the 2002 race. *Photo by Nancy L. Ford*

Opposite, top: **Leon Starowicz of Yorkville, N.Y., triumphantly crosses the finish line carrying the American flag in front of the F. X. Matt Brewery on Court Street in 2002.** *Photo by Michael Doherty*

Opposite, bottom: **A motorcycle provides a moving tripod for a video cameraman along the race course in 1994.** *Photo by Gary Fountain*

SARANAC
11874
BOILERMAKER 15K
ROAD RACE

Sam Russo wipes his brow as he directs the post-race party area cleanup in 2002. *Photo by Elizabeth A. Mundschenk*

From left to right, Jeff Ceria, Rebecca Ceria, Christi Sobel and Brenda Cartland massage each other's backs before the 2001 race. *Photo by Nancy L. Ford*

Runner Mary Leary of Cortland, N.Y., cools off after the hot run.
Photo by Heather Martin

Danny A. DeSimone of Morrisville, Pa., cools off in a sprinkler after finishing the 25th Boilermaker in 2002.
Photo by Elizabeth A. Mundschenk

Spectators watch runners make their way up Culver Avenue at the start of the 25th Boilermaker in 2002.
Photo by Angel E. Chevrestt

Boilermaker Race Course

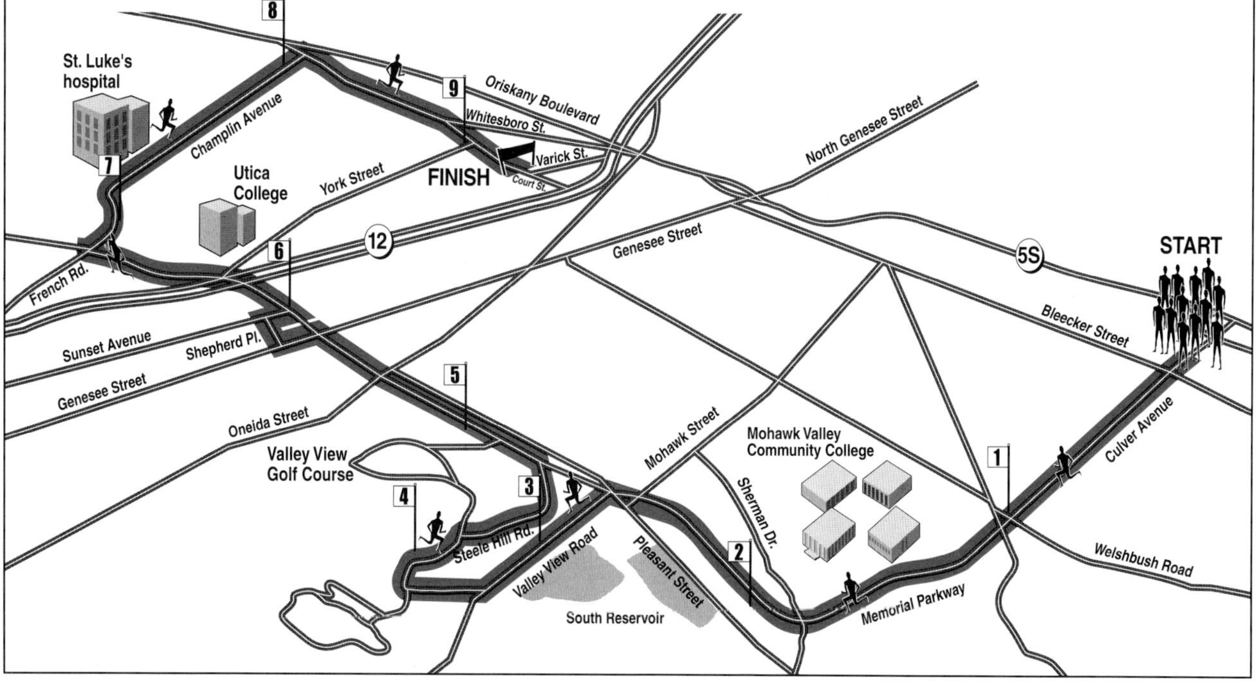

1978

1979

1980

1981

1982

1983

1984

1985

1986

1987

1988

1989

1990

1991

1992

1993

1994

1995

1996

1997

1998

1999

2000

2001

2002

Every runner receives a commemorative glass. *Photos by Elizabeth A. Mundschenk*

1993

Kenyan Role Solidifies

Thomas Osano was not the first Kenyan to win the Utica Boilermaker Road Race. Joseph Kipsang was the first native of the East African nation to grab the title, back in 1986, and he won again in 1988. And Sammy Lelei won the race in 1992.

Osano's victory on July 11, 1993, however, made it obvious the Kenyans were here to stay, in Utica, N.Y., and on road-racing courses throughout the United States. It was a development that was not greeted warmly by everyone, especially American runners who saw their earning power drop dramatically, but road-racing fans in Central New York had no problem with it. The Kenyans and other athletes from the running-mad African continent always have been made to feel welcome at the Boilermaker.

And they do feel welcome. In seventeen years through 2002, starting with Kipsang's 1986 victory, Kenyan men have won the race twelve times. They've won each year since 1992, except for 1998. That's when Khalid Khannouchi, who since has twice broken the world record in the marathon, won his title. And Khannouchi, while not a Kenyan, is an African, a native of Morocco who is now a United States citizen.

The Kenyan dominance extends to the women's side as well. Delillah Asiago was the first Kenyan to win the women's open, in 1994. Rosali Machado of Brazil won the next year, but from 1996 through 2001 the championship was won by either Catherine Ndereba (four times) or Lornah Kiplagat (twice), both Kenyans. Romania's Constantina Dita won in 2002.

And now, Kenyans are beginning to win in the masters division. Wilson Waigwa was the first in 1989. Peter Koech won in 1998 and Andrew Masai won in 2000, 2001 and 2002. No Kenyan women have won masters titles, probably only because none of international status has reached the required age of forty.

The Kenyans don't dominate only the Boilermaker, however. They win everywhere on the road-racing circuit. In 2001, three of the top four ranked women's road racers in the world were from Kenya, and the other was from South Africa. Four of the top seven men were from Kenya, two more were from Ethiopia and the other from Tanzania.

Kenyans—famous names like Paul Tergat and 2002 Boston Marathon champion Rodgers Rop among them—own the world's best men's times at every road race distance from 5 to 25 kilometers.

Why? It is a good question, with no simple answer.

Kenya and some of the other African nations have strong running traditions. Kenya's is based on the 1960s Olympic heroics of Kip Keino. There might be cultural factors, including the necessity to run to school and to do chores, even herd cattle, in early youth, and a propensity for hard work. Physiological factors, such as a tendency toward long-legged, light-boned physiques, might play a role. So, too, might be the fact that most of Kenya is far above sea level, leading to an advantage for runners when they race at lower altitudes.

Or the reason might just be hunger, both physical and psychological. "I think it is because they have a different lifestyle, running and walking to school," said Alec Riddle, an agent who represents South African runners. "I think they are

1993 HIGHLIGHTS

MEN
Thomas Osano
Kenya, 43:39

WOMEN
Gitte Karlshoj
Denmark, 51:07

MEN'S MASTERS
Nick Rose
Great Britain, 46:00

WOMEN'S MASTERS
Carol McLatchie
USA, 54:56

WHEELCHAIR MEN
Chris Waddell
USA, 41:41

WHEELCHAIR WOMEN
Connie Head
USA, 57:08

Men's winner Thomas Osano

Spectators watch from the sidelines at the 1993 Utica Boilermaker Road Race. *Photo by Elizabeth A. Mundschenk*

Edward B. Bradley of New Hartford, N.Y., pushed his way up the hill on Culver Avenue shortly after the start of the race. *Photo by Elizabeth A. Mundschenk*

prepared to sacrifice more and work harder. It's like the boxing thing. They're hungry."

"I don't think it is genetic," said Lisa Buster, who represents four-time Boilermaker winner Catherine Ndereba, the world record holder in the marathon. "They're tremendously dedicated, tremendously hardworking. When they come here [for the racing season], they are here to train and race. They don't do anything else."

Derek Froude, another agent who has managed just one or two Kenyans but has seen them win many races, has a succinct view. "I think that they begin with a genetic advantage to which they add a hunger to succeed and willingness to work as hard as necessary," he said.

Godfrey Kiprotich, a road-race veteran from Kenya who has run the Boilermaker several times, has said he and his countrymen have benefited from their hard work.

"It's training, all training," he said.

And the motivation for the training is obvious. "With the dollars you make here, that motivates the young [Kenyans]," he said in a 1998 Utica *Observer-Dispatch* story. "The average annual income in Kenya is about $300. A couple of thousand dollars can allow you to live comfortably for a year or two."

The Kenyan dominance of American road racing was so complete by the late 1990s that a backlash was created. Charges of racism were made—some said that if the Kenyans hadn't been black Africans no one would have cared—while others maintained that something had to be done to develop a rapidly atrophying American distance-running contingent.

One prominent race, Colorado's Bolder Boulder, went to an Olympic format—with three-man teams from foreign nations, but allowing unlimited American entries—and got a lot of negative press for doing so.

At the time, Bolder Boulder professional athlete coordinator Rich Castro said the idea was to promote American distance running, not discriminate against Kenyans or any other African runners.

"We were searching for a format where we could give the Americans some level of success and still have an international field," he told *Observer-Dispatch* Sports Editor Craig Muder. "We decided to adopt an Olympic format because we literally had no American entries. As it turned out, the American women finished sixth out of twelve teams and the men were seventh out of fourteen.

"In the end, the Kenyans won both individual titles and we had six African countries represented. So if we were doing this to limit the success of black African runners, we did a pretty poor job," Castro said.

The Boilermaker, however, took a firm stance in favor of an open race, with Earle Reed referring to complaints by American runners as "whining."

"The Kenyans just work harder, and they know what a prize of $5,000 means in Kenya," he said. "The Americans don't have that financial drive because the money doesn't go as far here."

American running legends Bill Rodgers and Frank Shorter felt that there had to be more emphasis on the sport in the United States for Americans to be successful and to be able to run with the Kenyans. Shorter thought subsidized prize money for Americans might help, but acknowledged there was more to it than that.

"Money just isn't enough motivation to make you train as hard as the Kenyans do," he said. "Running goals must be more important than money if Americans are to catch up. ... We support winners. If we

Dale Miller of Ilion, N.Y., runs through a spray of water during the race. *Photo by Elizabeth A. Mundschenk*

Gitte Karlshoj of Denmark breaks the tape to win the women's race. *Photo by Nancy L. Ford*

don't see our athletes win, we don't support the sport."

"To the Kenyans or Ethiopians or Moroccans, [running is] the national sport," Rodgers said. "It's kind of like Americans with football or baseball. Running or track and field is probably around fifteenth in national interest level here."

"Some people think it's just a matter of working hard. I don't believe that. The issue is a complex one. America has open arms and it should be true in sports," Rodgers said. "At the same time, you have the delicate issue that we are not able to produce all these top level runners because it is not a priority."

Benson Masya, who won the 1994 Boilermaker in a record time of 42:57, said after that victory he and his countrymen weren't hiding anything. "There is no secret," he said after burning up the course. "The ones who train hard do well."

Osano didn't care about any of the theories of Kenyan success or the problems of American runners. He just went out and ran.

The field included the previous three champions—Sammy Lelei (1992), Ed Eyestone (1991) and Delmir Dos Santos (1990)—but Osano had defeated Lelei at the Atlanta Peachtree Road Race in Georgia on July 4, and he had been running well throughout the season.

Running under a brilliant sun with the temperature rising minute by minute, eventually reaching the mid-80s by the time the bulk of the 4,966 runners finished, Osano kicked hard over the last half mile to equal Lelei's course record of 43:39. "My intention was to win this race," Osano said afterward. "I really came to win. I am so happy to win this race. I am very happy with what I have done."

After 5 miles, it was a two-man race: Osano and Lelei. Lelei knew he couldn't outkick Osano, so he tried to build a big lead on the downhills. He did build leads, but Osano stayed close, then caught and passed Lelei on Whitesboro Street. That all made sense. Osano didn't like downhills, Lelei did. Osano liked uphills, Lelei didn't. And Osano was faster on the flats, which is why he didn't worry about much of anything until the Whitesboro Street stretch.

Lelei, a tiny runner weighing just 114 pounds, thought he could still win as they cut into Court Street. No chance. Osano pounded down the stretch to the finish. Lelei was 6 seconds back.

Women's open winner Gitte Karlshoj had an easy road to victory, or at least as easy as Boilermakers get. She passed Russian Olympian Valentina Yegorova near the 6-mile mark and went on to finish in 51:07. Gordon Bloch also passed Yegorova and finished second in 51:46. Vernon Center, N.Y.'s Heidi Gerken was sixth in 52:50.

"I just felt great," Karlshoj said. "I wasn't tired a single second out there, and I don't know why. The pace was just right for me."

Karlshoj spent five days here before the race, staying with her friend Judy Owens in Sauquoit, N.Y., and even helped stuff race packets with Boilermaker volunteers the Thursday before the race.

Carol McLatchie won the women's masters race in record time, 54:56, despite the heat. Canada's Diane Legare, who would become a Boilermaker fixture and the 1994 and 1999 champion, was second.

McLatchie said she had no idea she was running a record pace. "It was so warm this morning, and it's such a long race that I decided I was just going to go out and see how I felt," she said. "I was just trying to finish. This is such a tough field."

England's Nick Rose won the men's masters race, running 46:00 to outdistance friendly rivals Manuel Vera of Mexico (46:35) and Nigel Gates, also of England (46:49).

Despite the heat, Chris Waddell, a twenty-four-year-old from Granby, Mass., set a men's wheelchair record in 41:41. "It's a good course," he said. "It seems more uphill than down, but the weather was fine. I thought it was a really comfortable race."

"I think they are prepared to sacrifice more and work harder."

—Alec Riddle, an agent, on why the Kenyans win

Bob Balk of Rochester, N.Y., was second in 47:23, not bad at all considering he had a flat tire.

Connie Head of Windsor, N.Y., won her third consecutive title in the women's wheelchair division in 57:08.

Jay Frisillo of New Hartford, N.Y., was the top local runner (50:36, thirty-fourth), although Brian Fullem, formerly of Utica, was thirtieth in 49:43 and Lance Denning, formerly of Oneida, N.Y., was thirty-first in the same time.

Tracey Bunce of Clinton, N.Y., ran 58:41, the best time among local women, and Hamilton College track and cross-country coach Ellen Hull was thirty-fifth in 1:00:14.

There were 4,966 entrants in the race and 4,243 finishers, both records.

Dappled sunlight streams through the trees, illuminating runners along the Utica, N.Y., race course. *Photo by Elizabeth A. Mundschenk*

Nick Morosco of Yorkville, N.Y., fills water cups at the Yorkville Fire Department's water station in 1994.
Photo by Elizabeth A. Mundschenk

1994

Kenyan Women Get into the Act

The Kenyan men already had conquered the Utica Boilermaker Road Race. By 1994, Kenyans had won the men's open title five times in nine years, and they would dominate the action even more as time went on.

Until then, however, no Kenyan woman had ever won — maybe because no Kenyan woman had even run the race.

Delillah Asiago took care of that on July 10. On a relatively cool, somewhat cloudy day that made for good running conditions, Asiago ran a 50:24, easily outdistancing Canadian Olympian Nancy Tinari (51:15) and introducing the era of Kenyan women at the Boilermaker.

Benson Masya, also of Kenya, won the men's race in one of the most dominant performances in Boilermaker history. He ran 42:57, 42 seconds better than the record set by Sammy Lelei in 1992 and equaled by Thomas Osano in 1993 and 37 seconds ahead of second-place finisher Lazarus Nyakeraka.

Canada's Diane Legare won her first women's masters title and Mexico's Martin Mondragon, the 1989 Los Angeles Marathon winner, won the men's masters crown. Former champion Nick Rose was second, the fourth time during the season he was runnerup to Mondragon.

Utica, N.Y., native Peter Pazik, a resident of Connecticut, was listed as the top local finisher, thirty-third in 47:56. Mike Bronson of Mohawk, N.Y., finished in 50:34. New Hartford, N.Y.'s Heather Fenton was the top local woman in 56:56.

While Masya's record run was remarkable, Asiago's victory, in retrospect, was the big news. It became a benchmark, not just for the Boilermaker, but for women's road racing in general. Although Tegla Loroupe's win in the New York City Marathon later that year often is regarded as the big breakthrough, Asiago's victory in Utica certainly was one of the earliest wins by a Kenyan on the American road-racing circuit.

Asiago, twenty-two at the time and a new mother for eight months, certainly wasn't thinking about historical significance when she came to Utica. She just wanted to win and earn the $5,000 top prize. "I was just in front from the beginning," she said after the race. "I got to the finish line and looked behind me and nobody was there."

Many Kenyan women followed Asiago to Utica, and they've been extremely successful. Rosali Machado of Brazil won the 1995 Boilermaker, but it was an all-Kenyan affair until Romania's Constantina Dita won in 2002.

Where were the Kenyan women before the early 1990s? Mostly at home. The culture generally did not support women taking off and running for a living.

Loroupe is considered the pioneer of the movement because winning New York was sensational news back home. In fact, when she returned, she was given gifts of sheep and cattle and, she told *Outside Magazine*, an ostrich feather—a trophy usually reserved for victorious warriors.

Loroupe had a typical rural childhood in Kenya, including running to and from school and herding farm animals on foot, which helped develop speed and stamina. She had been discouraged, however, from competitive running as a teenager. "When I ran in school, the men in my tribe said, 'Tegla, you're wasting your time,'" she was quoted as saying by coolrunning.com.

1994 HIGHLIGHTS

MEN
Benson Masya
Kenya, 42:57

WOMEN
Delillah Asiago
Kenya, 50:24

MEN'S MASTERS
Martin Mondragon
Mexico, 45:28

WOMEN'S MASTERS
Diane Legare
Canada, 55:38

WHEELCHAIR MEN
Chris Waddell
USA, 40:17

WHEELCHAIR WOMEN
Harrilyn Beehner
USA, 1:16:25

Men's winner Benson Masya

Women's winner Delillah Asiago

The start of the 1994 Boilermaker 15K as the more than 5,000 registered runners set off. *Photo by Gary Fountain*

Luckily, she didn't pay attention. By age twenty-two, she had won New York twice and later added the London and Berlin Marathons to her list of championships. Catherine Ndereba, the four-time Boilermaker champion, two-time Boston Marathon champion and world record holder in the marathon, regarded Loroupe as a heroine and role model, as do all female runners in Kenya. "They've seen Tegla Loroupe," she said before the 2002 Boston Marathon. "Each and every one is getting inspired."

Cooling down was not for just the racers. An unidentified spectator runs through the fire hydrant spray near the end of the finish-line chutes. *Photo by Elizabeth A. Mundschenk*

The success of the Kenyan men on the U.S. running circuit helped break barriers, said Lisa Buster, Ndereba's American agent. "With the success of the men, people started realizing what could happen," Buster said. "You had people who liked the sport, and they got involved. But in her town of Nyeri, people looked at her like she was crazy. It was not something that nice young ladies did, except that her father encouraged her. Now, it is changing. There are more role models. Before, it was, you got out the door and got married."

Kenyan women still get married and have children, but they run, too. While not as dominant as the men from Kenya, they certainly seem to be the single most successful group of female road racers in the world.

Women's marathon pioneer Kathrine Switzer is a great admirer of them. "The Kenyan women are very unique as they come from a society that expects them to marry and start a big family at about age sixteen," she said. "They work very hard and don't get a lot of respect. Thus, the women runners have a lifetime of an incredible work ethic, and are willing to suffer to obtain a goal.

"Uniquely, they are optimistic, bright, loving and usually very religious. Put this together with the fact that for generations, like the men, they are born and bred at altitude and also have to run or walk everywhere, they grow up very strong—basically, all the ingredients for being a good runner."

Kenyan women have used their winnings to improve the lives of their families, friends and fellow citizens, have encouraged young women to become involved in sports and basically shared the fruits of their talent and hard work. Switzer points out that this has earned them enormous respect, leading to honors as warriors such as those bestowed on Loroupe.

While women from Japan, South Africa, Italy, Eastern Europe and South America have done well in American road racing, the Kenyans still lead the pack. "The drive to succeed and need to succeed is great in all those countries, but right now none is greater than Kenya," Switzer said.

Asiago had little trouble outdistancing Tinari, a gold medal winner at 10,000 meters in the 1988 Olympics. Defending champion Gitte Karlshoj of Denmark had to drop out at 10 kilometers as her legs simply gave out.

Masya was all but unchallenged as well, cruising to one of the more unusual victories in Boilermaker history. The twenty-four-year-old Kenyan, a one-time boxer who had won the Peachtree Road Race 10K on July 4 in Atlanta, Ga., was picked by many, including U.S. Olympic hero Frank Shorter, to win in Utica.

"The women runners have a lifetime of an incredible work ethic."

—Kathrine Switzer, racing pioneer, on her admiration for female Kenyan runners

He didn't disappoint, running much of the race with his competition far, far behind. He easily blew up Lelei's and Thomas Osano's records and for a time threatened the then-world record of 42:37 for the 15-kilometer distance. "I wasn't thinking about that," he said after the race. "I didn't even know what the course record was. I just wanted to do better than last year."

In 1993, a tired Masya didn't arrive until very late Saturday and ran a 47:11 to finish a disappointing twentieth.

Florence Schreck, of Whitesboro, N.Y., second from left, shouts as she hands out cups of water at the Yorkville (N.Y.) Fire Dept. water station on Champlin Avenue during the 1994 Boilermaker. *Photo by Elizabeth A. Mundschenk*

Legare won the women's masters in her third attempt. The bubbly Montrealer got out front early and worked her way to a 55:38 finish for her tenth victory in eleven races to that point in 1994. "I wasn't sure I won until the finish line," she said. "I know most of the women, and I had a good feeling. I passed two or three others and was very positive."

Rose, the 1993 champion, couldn't get the best of Mondragon, who beat him by 13 seconds in Atlanta and also edged him in two other races. This time, Mondragon won in 45:28, with Rose far back in 46:25. "One day I'm going to rein him in," Rose said. "You never give up."

The race pushed over the 5,000-runner mark for the first time (5,105) and 4,466 finished.

One of the newcomers was Shorter, the 1972 Olympic gold medalist and 1976 silver medalist in the marathon. Shorter, forty-six, ran 57:43 to finish two hundred twentieth overall, and while he wasn't happy with his time, he enjoyed himself. "I got to know a lot of the people running around me, because all the spectators would call out their names," Shorter said, addressing the crowd at the post-race party. "It was great, there was a lot of community support." Shorter promised then he would return, and he has each year, with his appearance sponsored by the Petrone & Petrone law firm.

Chris Waddell of Granby, Mass., won the men's wheelchair race in 40:17. Harrilyn Beehner of Saratoga Springs, N.Y., won the women's title in 1:16:25.

James Menard (left) and Timothy Menard (right), both of Virginia Beach, Va., raise their arms as they approach the finish of the race. Running between them is William Evans of Rome, N.Y. *Photo by Bradford S. Luppino*

1995

Volunteers Play Prominent Role

By 1995, the Utica Boilermaker Road Race was a fully mature event. Already recognized as one of the top road races in the country by the media, and continuing to grow into the largest 15K race in the nation—which it became in 1997—it enjoyed a wonderful reputation among runners from across the country and around the world.

It also had solidified itself as the area's crown jewel, a social and athletic happening, a gigantic family reunion and street fair that had developed into perhaps the best advertisement the Utica-Rome, N.Y., area has ever had.

The July 9, 1995, race didn't hurt the process, with exciting races and record runs in the major divisions and an all-time high field of 5,506, with 4,763 finishers. The race was broadcast live and then on tape by both local television stations and was covered from every possible angle by almost every local radio station and print media outlet.

Lazarus Nyakeraka, just nineteen, won the men's open race in a dramatic finish with fellow Kenyan Joseph Kamau. Rosali Machado of Brazil won the closest women's race up to that time, outkicking Anne Hare to win by 3 seconds. New Zealand's Lorraine Moller ripped off a record 53:16 in winning the women's masters title, and Mexico's Martin Mondragon won the men's masters title a second straight time.

To top it all off, John Rodolph won the men's wheelchair title after duct-taping his chair back together on the advice of women's wheelchair winner Connie Head and with the assistance of Boilermaker volunteers Dave Jones, Bob McQueen and Jeff Adams.

Volunteers, in fact, had become a huge element in the Boilermaker's success. They numbered about 2,000 in 1995, and have since swelled to about 5,000. The Boilermaker wouldn't be the Boilermaker without them.

Some of the volunteers are former runners. Some have never run in their lives. Some have run just a little. Debbie Johncox, who has been the director of volunteers for about a decade, has run the race just once. "That was enough," she said with a laugh, recalling she ran with other committee members the week before the race. "I'm not really an avid runner."

But the avid runners couldn't get along without Johncox and her volunteers, who do everything they can to smooth things along, from passing out water at the more than twenty water stations along the course to pouring beer at the post-race party.

Volunteers also provide for entertainment, staff the finish line, process race applications, produce the awards ceremony, escort elite runners, direct the Youth Run, 8K Walk and 5K Training Run, put together the pre-race Expo, stuff goody bags, handle traffic and safety, do the clean-up, and on and on.

Why do they do it? "I think it's a sense of pride in the community and pride in this event," said Johncox, a volunteer for nearly twenty years. "They want to be associated with it. I know people who volunteer and this is the only community thing they do. They're proud to have family and friends come in and run the race."

There also are tangible benefits. Volunteers receive T-shirts and other merchandise, and there is an invitation-only party for them as well. That party now

1995 HIGHLIGHTS

MEN
Lazarus Nyakeraka
Kenya, 43:09

WOMEN
Rosali Machado
Brazil, 49:42

MEN'S MASTERS
Martin Mondragon
Mexico, 45:26

WOMEN'S MASTERS
Lorraine Moller
New Zealand, 53:16

WHEELCHAIR MEN
John Rodolph
USA, 42:56

WHEELCHAIR WOMEN
Connie Head
USA, 1:12:30

Men's winner Lazarus Nyakeraka

Women's winner Rosali Machado

Charlene Koughlin of Frankfort, N.Y., holds a sign encouraging her husband, Jack, as he runs in the 1995 race. *Photo by Nancy L. Ford*

takes place the Friday before the race. Johncox began directing it in 1994 in an effort to spur attendance. Only a few hundred volunteers used to attend the post-race party. "I found the enthusiasm died after the race," Johncox said. "This built the enthusiasm for getting out of bed on Sunday morning or working all day Saturday."

Mary Lou Rosencrants has been a volunteer since the very first run in 1978. Her husband, the late Steve Rosencrants, ran that first year, then took charge of coordinating the ham radio operators who help support the race and remained involved until his death in 1992. "My sister, my stepson, my brother-in-law, my niece and nephew-in-law are all volunteers," Rosencrants said. "It's a family event for all of us. It's a lot of fun and a way of getting into the community spirit. I originally became involved because my husband was interested and because Boilermaker founder Earle Reed is a friend. I can't imagine not doing it now."

Pam Hallack hugs her sister-in-law Mary Ann Serwatka after Hallack and her husband, Tom Serwatka, finished last. "They don't give you this kind of attention for finishing just anywhere," Hallack said. *Photo by Nancy L. Ford*

Mary Luker has been a volunteer since 1987 and is now in charge of entertainment on the course—disc jockeys and groups such as the Mohawk Valley Frasers bagpipers. "We have two or three units per mile," said Luker, who runs the race every year herself since her work is done by race time. "I've never seen anything like it in any other race. It seems like everybody comments about the zoo animals. They bring them down to the course. And the bagpipers are very popular. They've been out there ten years now, and I still get the chills."

Luker volunteers in part because she feels it is a big boost for the Utica area—and because she has a lot of fun. "I'm a born and raised Utican," she said. "I love the race, and it is a wonderful way to promote the community. It's a great time and it still hasn't gotten old. It gives everyone a reason to party. That one Sunday in July is a blast."

Like many volunteers, Cosmo Castellano isn't a runner. "I couldn't run from here to the parking lot," he said, but he has been involved in the race for many years and has headed the Corporate Cup committee for the last decade.

His wife, Nancy, is co-chairman, and she is a runner—a good one, too, having done 1:04:03 one year.

The Corporate Cup is a competition among area businesses that, Castellano said, has become a race within a race. There are large, medium and small classifications, and masters, coed, male and female divisions. "I've always enjoyed doing it," Castellano said. "For a lot of volunteers, it's like a family thing. It's really a neat thing to do, especially when we have our awards ceremony. It really puts a face on our local business people. You meet these guys, and it gives a lot of exposure to local business."

Because the volunteers are so important to the race, the organizers do their best to take care of them. The party and T-shirts help, and each volunteer has his or her name listed in the Utica *Observer-Dispatch*. And, each year, an outstanding volunteer is honored with the Peter DeStefano Award, named for the late Utica (N.Y.) Free Academy coach and athletic director who was a dedicated volunteer in the early years of the race. Johncox, Castellano and Rosencrants are among the past winners.

The runners enjoyed the 1995 Boilermaker more than most, since relatively low temperatures—about 70° at race time—and a very light breeze made for pleasant conditions. Dr. Michael Garrett, the race's longtime medical director, credited the weather with keeping injuries to a minimum.

"There was no wind, no humidity; we ran at our best," said nineteen-year-old Lazarus Nyakeraka, who had finished second in 1994.

Nyakeraka and Kamau outdueled England's Peter Whitehead and South Africa's Simon Morolong, then went shoulder-to-shoulder in the last few hundred yards down Court Street.

By that time, the $70,000 bonus for a 15K road-race world record that had been put up by Utica's WIBX radio and Blue Cross/Blue Shield of Utica/Watertown was out of the question. The early miles had been far too slow.

"I did not think of it," Nyakeraka said. "When we reached halfway, I focused on winning."

A gaffe by Kamau helped him do that. The two of them were flying down the stretch when Kamau began to veer across the course, apparently following the media

Todd E. Scott gives Teresa Scott a gentle push across the finish line at the end of the long race. *Photo by Elizabeth A. Mundschenk*

Runners pass a water station during the 15K (9.3-mile) race. *Photo by Elizabeth A. Mundschenk*

truck that had turned down Stark Street, a block from the finish.

Nyakeraka just kept motoring to the line, winning in 43:09, with the confused Kamau 3 seconds back. Some thought Kamau's error cost him the race; others disagreed. He thought it probably did, but refused to blame anyone else. "I was determined to win, but I accept the result," he said.

Dick Mattia, the Boilermaker's coordinator of elite runners, felt Nyakeraka had begun his strong kick before Kamau veered off and would have won in any case. He also mentioned that all the elite runners were offered tours of the course, and he didn't think Kamau took one.

"I think it's a sense of pride in the community and pride in this event."

—Debbie Johncox, longtime volunteer, on why people pitch in

"I've had a couple of runners say they don't like to see the course beforehand, although I don't know why," Mattia said at the time. "If you want to play your strategy, you have to see it. If I'm wrong and he saw the course, I think it was a lack of concentration on his part."

The women's race also came down to a late sprint, with Machado edging New Zealand's Hare by three seconds—49:42 to 49:45—in the closest finish up to that point.

Machado came to the race expecting to win, but found it was tougher than she imagined. "This was a very competitive race, not just at the finish, but all the way through," she said, speaking through an interpreter. "We were always neck-and-neck, shoulder-to-shoulder."

The race came down to the bitter end. "I felt like I had a shot at her," Hare said. "She just happened to be a little stronger the last couple hundred yards."

South Africa Olympian Colleen De Reuck was third and Kim Jones of Spokane, Wash., was fourth.

Moller had been a bronze medal winner in the marathon in the 1992 Olympics, a month or so after she had placed sixth in her first Boilermaker in 52:37. This time, at age forty, she ran 53:16, setting a women's masters record.

It was Moller's fifth race in as many weeks, and she said her body had been telling her to take a break. "But this race is so fantastic to come to," she said. "I'm glad I came because it's more than just a race. It's a community event and it's really fun to be part of it."

Chris Getman of Ilion, N.Y., and Syracuse University was the top local men's runner (49:12) and Heather Fenton of New Hartford, N.Y., and Wilmington, N.C., (56:20) was the top local woman.

The race continued to exhibit its unusual spirit in many ways. Among them: Running legend and former Boilermaker champion Bill Rodgers won $200 in the masters division, then gave half of it to the Operation Sunshine Campership Fund—an *Observer-Dispatch* charity—and half to the Salvation Army.

Rodolph, who still had to nearly come to a stop at every turn, won the wheelchair race in 42:56. Head won the women's division in 1:12:30.

Jean Allaire of Utica, N.Y., leads cheers for her son, Andy, as he nears the finish line. Andy had his right leg amputated following a 1988 motorcycle accident. While recovering at St. Elizabeth's hospital he told nurses he would one day run in the Boilermaker. In 1995 race organizers awarded him the Bill Coughlin Award, given each year to a runner who shows exemplary courage. *Photo by Elizabeth A. Mundschenk*

Racers in the wheelchair division get under way at the 1996 Utica Boilermaker Road Race. *Photo by Elizabeth A. Mundschenk*

Kyle R. Stephenson of Richmond, Va., sprints toward the finish line. *Photo by Elizabeth A. Mundschenk*

1996

Older Runners Strong in the Pack

1996 HIGHLIGHTS

MEN
Joseph Kimani
Kenya, 42:40
(race record)

WOMEN
Catherine Ndereba
Kenya, 48:55

MEN'S MASTERS
Karel Jircik
Canada, 47:29

WOMEN'S MASTERS
Tatyana Pozdnyakova
Ukraine, 52:03

WHEELCHAIR MEN
Tony M. Nogueira
USA, 36:15

WHEELCHAIR WOMEN
Rose Winand
USA, 46:08

The 1996 Boilermaker was graced by what was considered its most elite field to date. And it lived up to expectations that July 14. Kenya's Joseph Kimani won the men's open race in 42:40, still the fastest time ever although no longer the record because the course was rerouted the next year. Countrywoman Catherine Ndereba won in Utica, N.Y., for the first time, on her way to staking her claim as "Queen of the Boilermaker" when she won three consecutive times from 1999 through 2001.

The race pulled in a record 6,400 entrants—5,566 finished—and also continued to be a magnet for older runners from the Mohawk Valley and throughout Central New York.

Hundreds of runners in their sixties and older run the Boilermaker every year. It all started with Utican Lou Roberts, who ran the inaugural race in 1:07:00 minutes at age seventy-four. Two years later, Roberts got his time down to 1:38:42.

Roberts was the first of many "mature" Boilermaker runners. Among those local participants who ran well in 1996 were sixty-year-old Wayne Decker of Utica (1:03:36); Connie LaSalle of Whitesboro, N.Y., (1:22:43 in the women's 60-90 age group); Sam Gratch of Utica (1:30:07 in the men's 70-90); and Becky Morris of New Hartford, N.Y., (1:18:14 in the women's 55-59).

Decker, LaSalle and Gratch were three of the twenty-one runners who ran all of the first twenty-four Boilermakers. Morris also was still running strong heading into 2002. Some of the other standout local older runners over the years have been Dolores Quinn, Tom Hovey, Howard Rubin, Ed Buckley, Joseph Agone, Paul Ohlbaum, Dan Cohen and John Rastani.

Although he wasn't strictly speaking a local runner, the granddaddy of them all might have been Charlie Hackenheimer, from nearby Central Square, N.Y. He ran a sensational 1:17:40 at age seventy-nine in 1985, and was eighty-four when he ran a 1:51:16 in his final Boilermaker in 1990.

Hackenheimer, now deceased, owned numerous national road-race records in several age groups. The Syracuse (N.Y.) Chargers Track Club named its most outstanding male masters runner award for him. "Charlie was a tremendous person," said Chargers' president Dave Oja. "Gracious, unassuming, friendly and always cheerful."

Some of the older runners were track and cross-country stars in their high school and college days, but many of them didn't take up the sport until they were much older. Buckley began running at age forty-nine to alleviate a health problem, and ran the inaugural Boilermaker at age fifty-seven. "I don't think I'd even be around if I hadn't taken up running when I did," he said.

> *"I don't think I'd even be around if I hadn't taken up running when I did."*
> *—Boilermaker senior runner Ed Buckley*

Buckley, who has won many races and collected numerous awards, ran his best time of 1:01:18 in 1981, a month short of his sixtieth birthday. He missed the 2001 race after suffering a heart attack, but ran 1:28:47 in 2000.

Women's winner
Catherine Ndereba

Right: **The start of the 1996 race as seen through a fish-eye lens.** *Photo by Elizabeth A. Mundschenk*

Gratch, seventy-seven, also started running late, at forty-six, but has run more than one hundred thirty marathons since—Boston twenty-six times—and every Boilermaker until the 25th, when he was sidelined by a traffic accident. He has run the race in under 60 minutes.

Quinn began running in her early fifties, a couple of years before the Boilermaker began. "My husband [Ed] was running at the time, and he kind of talked me into it," she said.

Denise M. Hollenbeck, left, of Remsen, N.Y., crosses the finish line along with Mary E. Thorp of Plattsburgh, N.Y. *Photo by Elizabeth A. Mundschenk*

But Ed Quinn never ran the Boilermaker. "He launched me and then he stopped," Dolores Quinn said.

Quinn has no intention of stopping, despite having a heart pacemaker implanted and twice breaking her hip in recent years. She won many of her age group titles in the early days of the race.

What is the best thing about running? "The friends I've made since I've started," Quinn said. "A great new bunch of friends."

And what does she like about the Boilermaker? "The crowds, the excitement, just being a part of it," she said.

Grace McNasser, sixty-three, calls Quinn a terrific role model. "A wonderful inspiration for me and other runners," said McNasser, who has been running for about thirty years and is a pretty good role model herself. She has placed high in her age group several times, but she can't tell you what her best time is.

"I don't know," she said, then remembered it was about 83 minutes. "It's something I do; I love it because it is such a community event—the camaraderie, the training runs. It's just a great experience to be part of it. I run other races. I've done Gasparilla in Tampa, Fla. It cannot compare as far as the community spirit. You just can't beat the people lining the streets, the bands. There is no other race that is as great as the Boilermaker. People know it all over the country."

Howard Rubin is another top older runner. He's won his age group in the Boilermaker on several occasions, ripped off a 53:48 when he was fifty-five years old, and ran the race in 1:15:00 in 2000, when he was seventy-two. Unlike many of his peers, Rubin got his start at a young age, and was the Connecticut and New England champion in the half-mile in 1946. He ran in the Air Force, too, then dropped out for fifteen years before returning to the track and roads at age forty. "It's an integral part of my life," he said. "I look forward to the running and competing and hope I can do it the rest of my life."

Morris has been running for more than thirty years and has been in the top three in her age group in the Boilermaker many times. She won the women's masters division outright in 1980 with a time of 1:09:27, and she finished third in the 60-65 age group in 2001. Her husband, Bob, is one of the members of the elite group who has run in every Boilermaker. "We mainly started for physical fitness, and it was inexpensive," Morris said. "The Boilermaker is just one awesome race. It is so well run, the people are so enthusiastic. You are motivated by that, and your goals, by my husband running all of them. It's keeping on, keeping going for as long as our bodies can do it."

Kimani and Ndereba topped an extremely distinguished elite road-racing group that started at the head of the record field in the 1996 race. Dick Mattia, the elite runner coordinator for the Boilermaker, called it the deepest international field ever, and predicted that some records would fall.

Kimani, who had set a world road-race record at 10 kilometers in his victory at Atlanta, Georgia's Peachtree Road Race ten days before, headed a men's open field that included 1993 Boilermaker champion Thomas Osano; 1995 champion Lazarus Nyakeraka; Joseph Kamau, who was second to Nyakeraka that year; Simon Rono, second to Kimani at Peachtree; Khalid Khannouchi, who would win the 1998 Boilermaker and later set world marathon records in Chicago and London; and U.S. Olympian Mark Coogan.

In addition to Ndereba, the women's open field included Delillah Asiago, who in 1994 became the first Kenyan woman to win the Boilermaker and who won nine American road races in 1995; former child prodigy and Olympian Zola Budd-Pieterse of South Africa, who ran to fame as a barefoot teenager in the 1980s; 1993 Boilermaker champion Gitte Karlshoj of Denmark; 1996 Peachtree winner Hellen

Joseph Kimani of Kenya runs along Valley View Road on his way to victory in 1996. Kimani set a course record of 42 minutes and 40 seconds as he dominated the field.
Photo by Nancy L. Ford

Patricia J. Matrulli of Utica, N.Y., and Charles T. Zuis of Schuyler Lake, N.Y., complete the race hand-in-hand, the last finishers of the 1996 race, with times of 2:26:29 (Zuis) and 2:26:30 (Matrulli). "We met on the course and we were keeping an eye on each other," Matrulli said. "Then when we were approaching the finish line, he told me if I wanted to go ahead and cross the finish alone, to go ahead. I said, 'We've come this far, we're going to finish together.'" *Photo by Nancy L. Ford*

Kimaiyo-Kipkosgei of Kenya; former U.S. Olympian Gwyn Coogan; and New Hartford native Cheri Goddard, who ran the 5,000 meters in the U.S. Olympic trials the previous month.

The masters field was loaded, too. It included two-time defending champion Martin Mondragon of Mexico and racing legend and 1983 men's open champion Bill Rodgers, plus 1993 women's masters champion Carol McLatchie.

Kimani left little to chance on a day that began with a 68° start-time temperature but quickly grew in heat and humidity. After a mile and a half, he kissed everyone goodbye and took off on his own. "I wanted to break the world record," he said.

The mark at the time was 42:13, held by fellow Kenyan Paul Tergat. He didn't get that, but his 42:40 sliced 17 seconds off the Boilermaker mark set by Benson Masya in 1994. Kimani earned $5,000 to win and a $1,000 bonus for the record and no one has ever run a faster time, although his is no longer considered the course record because four turns were thrown into the course when it had to be adjusted to accommodate a starting line that was moved up 360 yards.

Kimani ran 42:54 in 1977 on the new course and that remained the record through 2002. "I didn't want to go in front early, but the pace was too slow," he said.

Kimani averaged 4:35 per mile for 9.3 miles—a fact that stunned Boilermaker fans who had any inkling of what it takes to run a mile that fast even once. He led by 120 yards at 4 miles, ran a 4:16 fifth mile and was so far ahead by the time he hit Oneida Street and then Genesee Street that fans couldn't make out anyone behind him and seemed bewildered that he arrived at those points so quickly.

A 4:49 seventh mile and a 5:02 ninth ruined any chance he had of getting the world record, but everything else was his, as Rono finished 29 seconds behind.

Ndereba, then twenty-three and still a few years removed from her glory days in the Boilermaker and at Boston and Chicago, won the women's open in 48:55. Nadia Prasad of France was second in 50:08. Budd-Pieterse was third in 50:15, and gave the Boilermaker her unqualified endorsement. "It was a great race," she said. "It's probably the best race I've ever run in."

Karel Jircik, a native Czech living in Toronto, upset Mondragon in the men's masters, running a 47:29, and Tatyana Pozdnyakova of the Ukraine won the women's masters race in a torrid 52:03, 73 seconds better than the record Lorraine Moller set in 1995. Pozdnyakova's time remained the record until Romania's Elena Fidatov ran 52:01 in 2002.

Tony Nogueira won the men's wheelchair division in 36:15, with Rose Winand winning the women's race in 46:08.

Peter Pazik of Utica was the top local men's runner in 48:22. Jeremy Burt of Hamilton, N.Y., ran 49:21. Kimberly Brady of Rome, N.Y., was the top local woman in 1:00:20.

1997

Setting the Pace on the 20th Birthday

Some road races start big and then peter out. Some start small and stay that way. Some trundle along, remaining modest but efficient, doing the important work of providing runners with competition and a forum in which to test their skills.

And some just grow into monsters—big, all-consuming, long-lived, generally benign monsters that get better with age.

The Boilermaker probably fits best into the last category. By 1997, the race was ready to celebrate its 20th running by aiming to become the largest 15-kilometer road race in America.

It did that, with 7,661 of the 9,458 entrants finishing on race day, July 13.

And it celebrated in a big way. Joseph Kimani won the men's open race in 42:54 over a slightly reconfigured course, and the time is still the course record. Fellow Kenyan Lornah Kiplagat outkicked countrywoman Hellen Kimaiyo-Kipkosgei to win by 2 seconds in the closest women's

1997 HIGHLIGHTS

MEN
Joseph Kimani
Kenya, 42:54
(course record)

WOMEN
Lornah Kiplagat
Kenya, 49:58

MEN'S MASTERS
Martin Mondragon
Mexico, 46:47

WOMEN'S MASTERS
Joan Benoit Samuelson
USA, 53:23

WHEELCHAIR MEN
Saul Mendoza
USA, 34:05

WHEELCHAIR WOMEN
Jessica Galli
USA, 52:18

Volunteers offer runner Alphonce Muindi of Kenya a drink as he charges toward the finish line of the 1997 Utica Boilermaker Road Race. *Photo by Heather Martin*

Men's winner Joseph Kimani

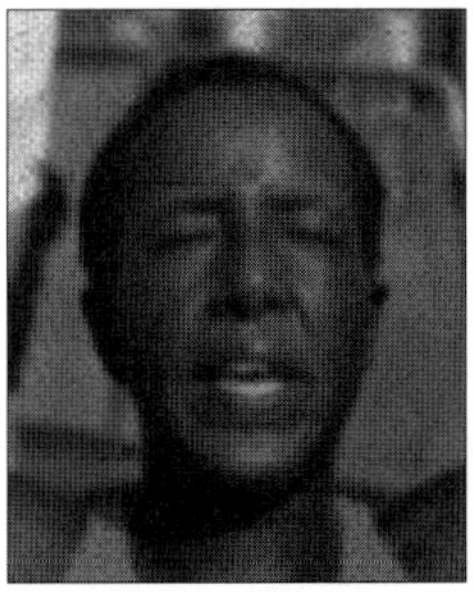

Women's winner Lornah Kiplagat

finish ever—until Kiplagat edged Jane Omoro by a second the next year.

There are other longtime races in the area. The Cazenovia (N.Y.) Fourth of July Foot Race, which includes a 10-mile run around Cazenovia Lake, began in 1973 and is believed to be the oldest road race in Central New York. The Utica (N.Y.) Roadrunners' Falling Leaves Race dates to 1975, the Syracuse YMCA Mountain Goat races celebrated their 25th birthday in 2002, and the JP Morgan Chase Corporate Challenge in Syracuse, N.Y., has been run for more than twenty years.

Other races were successful for some time and then died, such as the Diet Pepsi 10K in Liverpool, N.Y., and the Syracuse Freihofer's Run for Women.

As a result, the Boilermaker's 20th running was an important landmark for those who put the race together. To them, it certified that the race was fully mature, that it was going to be around for a long time, that it was a quality event.

"It was an opportunity," said former *Observer-Dispatch* running columnist Joe Kelly who was the race's assistant director. "We were taking advantage the way the Boston Marathon took advantage of their 100th birthday in 1996. You know the media was going to be interested. They are any time there is a significant anniversary. You want to make it a special time. We always wanted to have something every year, kind of an added thing, so the race wouldn't be a stagnant thing."

One of the benefits of reaching twenty years, Kelly said, was the ability to spark interest from new runners and rekindle the interest of former runners. "You get people saying, 'I've got to run the race again because it's the 20th,'" Kelly said. "Then you'll get new people saying, 'Well, gee, I've always wanted to run.' It's a little extra thing to get people off the dime. We take advantage, in a good way."

Earle Reed loved the idea that the race he founded had been around for two decades. "It was extremely gratifying, and it also is a classic study in a good marketing strategy," he said. "We had a whole bunch of satisfied customers for

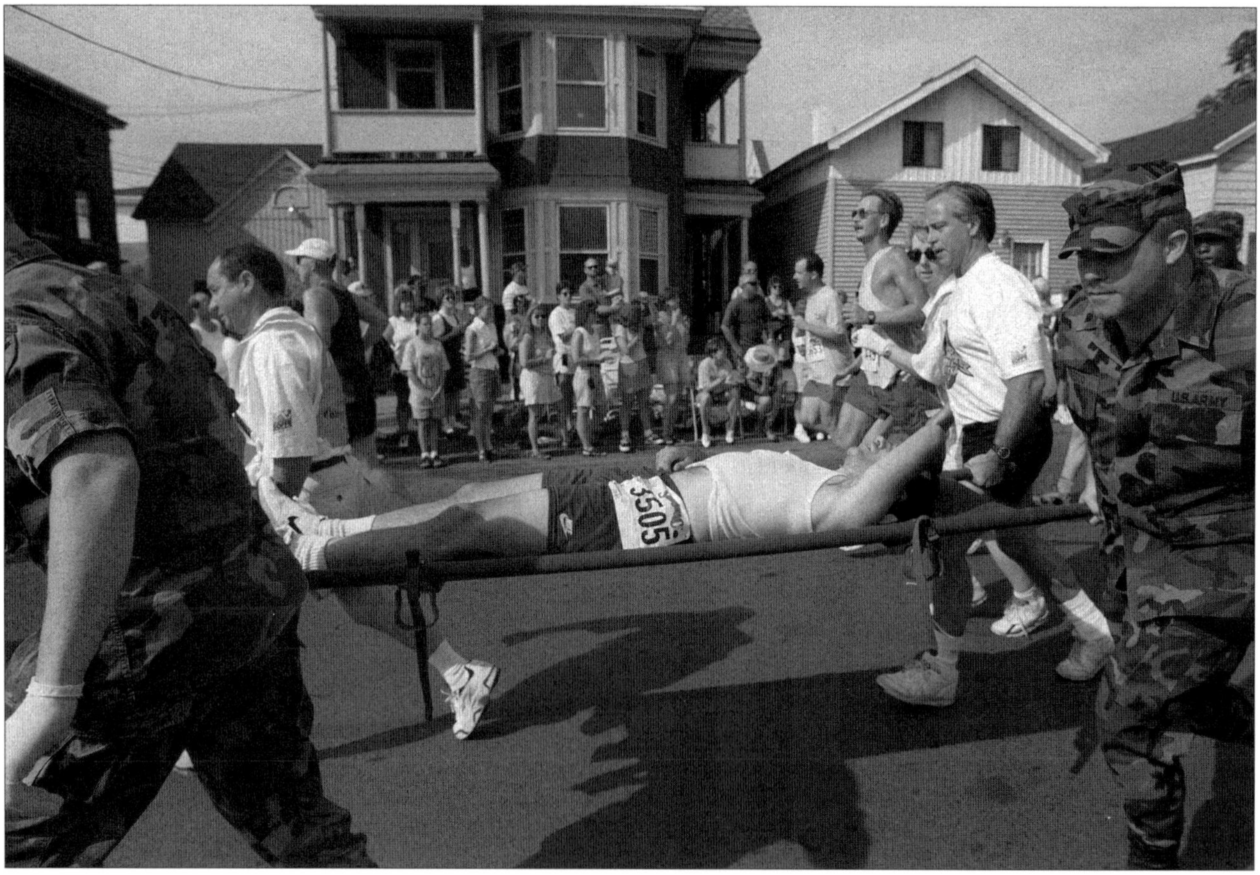

National Guard members carry David Gymburch of Lee Center, N.Y., to the finish line of the 1997 Boilermaker. *Photo by Nancy L. Ford*

nineteen years. They continued to sing the message and they brought more people with them."

Reed said that one of the reasons the Boilermaker had continued to grow and maintain its strong reputation is that the race responded well to constructive criticism. If the attitude wasn't exactly "the customer is always right," he feels it was something close to that. "Whenever we had a problem, like runners backing up in the chutes, we addressed it," he said. "We always tried to be responsive to our customers, our runners."

Being around for twenty years is an achievement unto itself. So is being the biggest, at least in most ways. The Boilermaker had no pretensions about becoming the largest 15K in the world—Italy's Stramilano draws more than 45,000 runners each year—but shooting for 10,000 entrants seemed reasonable.

Reed and Kelly didn't hit their goal, but the 9,458 entrants in 1997 were more than 3,000 more than the previous high in 1996. "Some people didn't want the race to grow that much," Kelly said. "I always wanted it to be the biggest 15K in the country.

"My thought was, if we could become the biggest in the United States, it would give us something to hang our hats on. It's good to be able to tell potential sponsors you are the biggest race in the country, and it's good for the runners. People who aren't runners don't necessarily know the quality of the race. How do you get that across? One of the ways is to have the biggest 15K in the country. All of a sudden people's eyes open up wide."

In truth, the 15K distance is relatively rare in American road racing. There simply aren't that many 15K races. The Boilermaker's chief competition is the Gate River Run in Jacksonville, Fla., in March—it's the USA Track & Field 15K championship—and the Gasparilla Distance Classic in Tampa, Fla., in February. Gate River held the title of the largest 15K until the 1997 Boilermaker passed it.

Reed thinks "the biggest" designation is a plus for the community. "This area lacks self-confidence, and that is what we are selling with the Boilermaker," he said. "We are giving people something to be proud of."

Some changes had to be made to accommodate all the additional runners. Dave Reichert and starting-line coordinator Jeff Adams moved the starting line up 360 yards to the south. That allowed room for more runners, and reduced the tunnel effect as runners came off the four-lane Route 5S ramp and squeezed onto the two-lane Culver Avenue.

Walter J. Rudy of Liverpool, N.Y., photographs runners along Champlin Avenue. Rudy, who wore a "runnercam" while participating, planned to share the video with friends from the Syracuse (N.Y.) Chargers running club.
Photo by Elizabeth A. Mundschenk

Runners make their way along Culver Avenue near Proctor Park shortly after the start of the race.
Photo by Elizabeth A. Mundschenk

Moving up the starting line meant the course had to be adjusted in some way, because the finish line on Court Street in front of the F.X. Matt Brewery wasn't going to be moved anytime soon.

> *"We had a whole bunch of satisfied customers for 19 years."*
>
> *—Boilermaker's Earle Reed, on the 20th race*

A jog was thrown into the course where it crossed Genesee Street, almost 6 miles into the race. Instead of crossing Genesee, the course now turned left onto Genesee for one block, right onto Shepherd Place, right onto Sunset Avenue and left onto Burrstone Road, resuming the original course.

Actually, it wasn't the first time the course had been reconfigured. The original start was near the intersection of Culver Avenue and Dwyer Avenue. It was pushed back to the Route 5S ramp in 1985, when The Athletics Congress established a new certification process. Turns, for example, had to be measured along the shortest possible route, so the starting line had to be pushed back 399 feet to make the course exactly 15 kilometers.

Because of the change, all the winners' times in 1997 would be course records. However, outstanding performances—like Kimani's 42:40 in 1996 and Jill Hunter's 48:19 in 1991—continued to be highly regarded and often were referred to as "race records."

The new course, with four new turns, might have been a touch slower than the original, although the streamlined starting area probably made up for whatever minimal time deficit the turns might have caused.

The turns certainly didn't bother Kimani or Kiplagat. Kimani, who had run away from a tough field the year before, cruised to victory again, becoming the first back-to-back men's open winner. The race was a near carbon copy of 1996. Kimani, twenty-five, rolled along off to the side of a large pack, then took off near Mohawk Valley Community College, 2 miles into the race.

He said afterward he thought the early pace was too slow. "I was looking at my watch," he said. "You don't want to run a bad time, so I decided to make my move."

As Godfrey Kiprotich said, everyone else was left with one option—to try hard to finish second. Peter Githuka was second in 43:21, Simon Sawe third in

43:33 and Kiprotich fourth in 43:41.

Kiplagat, who won the Los Angeles Marathon in March, had finished seventh in Atlanta's Peachtree 10K when she suffered in the heat. The milder weather in Utica—66° and clouds at race time, although the sun came out and heat increased as the race went on—helped as she battled Kimaiyo-Kipkosgei and 1994 champion Delillah Asiago. They were together most of the race, but Kiplagat kicked away the last half mile, then nearly ruined everything by following a media motorcycle off the course for a moment.

"I thought, 'I'm not going to win,'" she said. "But I was still very strong. I said, 'Okay, let me once again be strong.'"

Kiplagat was, holding off Kimaiyo-Kipkosgei, 49:58 to 50:00, with Asiago 7 seconds further back.

Kiplagat, who would win again in 1998, is a native of the village of Kipkapus, the home of many very good runners. "I was not a hero there," she said after her victory, "but I will be among them now."

American Joan Benoit Samuelson, winner of the first-ever women's Olympic marathon in 1984 ran the race for the first time and won the women's masters title handily, finishing in 53:23, with Regina Joyce of Lyndwood, Wash., second in 54:36.

Another homemade sign along the sidelines encourages runners competing in the 1997 race. *Photo by Nancy L. Ford*

"It was an honest and fair course," Samuelson said. "It was a smooth start. I was a little apprehensive because there were so many runners chomping at the bit. That's one of my biggest worries with races today."

Mexico's Martin Mondragon won his third men's masters title in four years, running 46:47 to best Ted Jaleta of Regina, Saskatchewan.

Bill Rodgers, the 1983 Boilermaker champion, was sixth in the masters

Competitors in the wheelchair division race through a hilly section of the 15K event. *Photo by Elizabeth A. Mundschenk*

The 1997 Utica Boilermaker Road Race gets underway. *Photo by Heather Martin*

in 49:36. His contemporary and 1972 Olympic hero Frank Shorter ran 57:15 to finish two hundred twentieth overall. "Out of the money, but I finished ahead of all the women," Rodgers laughed. "That's good."

Sam Mendoza of Snellville, Ga., won the men's wheelchair race in 34:05. Jessica Galli, just thirteen, won the women's race in 52:18.

Marcy, N.Y.'s Chris Sisting was the top Mohawk Valley woman in the field, finishing in 55:42 after being paced much of the way by her brother John, who ran 55:11. Marcus Gage of Mohawk, N.Y., (47:24); Chris Getman of Ilion, N.Y., (48:46); and Kyle Fenton of New Hartford, N.Y., (49:54) all got in under the 50-minute mark.

Tim Willis, twenty-six, a blind runner from Tucker, Ga., raced as a guest of the Central Association for the Blind and Visually Impaired, and finished in a very hot 53:30, one hundred fourth overall. Willis, a former varsity runner at Georgia Southern University who had raced all over the world and owned several world records for blind runners, ran with his guide and former coach, Jim Vargo. His time—he said beforehand he hoped to run between 52 and 54 minutes—immediately became a national record for a blind runner, since none had been established to that time for 15 kilometers.

Willis, a practicing attorney in Georgia, is now a recreational runner. He ran the 2002 Boilermaker.

The race also had a visit from endurance runner Helen Klein, seventy-four, who led a senior's walk at Acacia Village, a senior community on the grounds of the Masonic Home in Utica.

In another couple of firsts, the Boilermaker's Health & Fitness Expo was moved to the Masonic Home from its original home at the Riverside Mall, and was extended to two days. The annual Youth Run moved there, too.

The race's twentieth birthday was special, indeed, and hinted that the Boilermaker would be around for a long, long time to come.

"When I'm gone and you're gone and a lot of other people are gone, the race is still going to be here," Kelly said. "That gives me a lot of satisfaction. There is no question in my mind that seventy-five years from now, there is going to be a race called the Boilermaker, and it's going to be celebrating its 100th anniversary. It's going to be an institution, like the Boston Marathon."

Leprechaun Bill Corrigan of the Utica, N.Y., area throws happiness from his pot o' gold at runners. "It's exciting," Corrigan said. *Photo by Nancy L. Ford*

Bill Rodgers makes his acceptance speech at the first National Distance Running Hall of Fame induction ceremony at Hamiliton College on Saturday, July 11, 1998. In the back to the right is Bill's brother, Charlie. Joe Kelly, then director of the Hall of Fame, is at left. *Photo by Nancy L. Ford*

1998

Birth of the Hall of Fame

Khalid Khannouchi won, and would go on to set a world record in the marathon the next year. Lornah Kiplagat earned her second straight women's championship, this one by just one second.

What really distinguished the July 12, 1998, Boilermaker Road Race, however, was the fact that it was part of a weekend that included the induction of the first members of the National Distance Running Hall of Fame in Utica, N.Y.

Olympians Bill Rodgers, Frank Shorter, Joan Benoit Samuelson, Ted Corbitt and women's running pioneer Kathrine Switzer were honored as the first members of the Hall of Fame in ceremonies at Hamilton College (Clinton, N.Y.) on the eve of the 21st Boilermaker.

> *"They are going to look right here for their spiritual center."*
>
> *—Boilermaker announcer Phil Stewart, on the need for a Hall of Fame*

They would eventually be enshrined in a refurbished turn-of-the-century building in downtown Utica. "There are thirty million runners in America," said Boilermaker announcer Phil Stewart, a race director and outstanding road racer himself. "They are going to look right here for their spiritual center."

The effort to start the Hall of Fame had begun nearly a year before, and reached a crescendo when the city of Utica sold the 100-year-old building to the new group and then provided $100,000 in Federal Community Development Block Grant funds to upgrade the premises. Earle Reed and Utica Mayor Edward Hanna then kicked off the private drive for more funds with contributions of $5,000 each.

It was hoped the project would help revitalize Utica's downtown area, provide the Boilermaker with its own headquarters and tie in with other halls of fame, such as the Boxing Hall of Fame in Canastota, N.Y., the National Baseball Hall of Fame in Cooperstown, N.Y., and the Soccer Hall of Fame in Oneonta, N.Y.

The idea of the National Distance Running Hall of Fame was a hit with the inaugural class. "It gives our sport a way to speak to everybody, not just the runners," said Rodgers, who, along with Shorter, was given much of the credit for fueling the running boom of the 1970s. "It will highlight and showcase the athletes and people who make the sport strong. Road racing is a pretty darn strong sport throughout the world. We have a terrific record of success in road racing. You need a place to showcase that."

Rodgers said he hoped the Hall of Fame would help inspire younger runners. "You have young athletes looking up to other athletes," he said. "That's a powerful, powerful thing. It's a lot of fun. It's just such a high-energy thing. To have all those people highlighted and supported, I think that is fantastic. It needed to be done. This is a great way to get people's attention."

The original class has since been joined by a string of the great names in the sport—Francie Larrieu Smith, Nina Kuscsik, Billy Mills, Johnny Kelley, Steve

1998 HIGHLIGHTS

MEN
Khalid Khannouchi
Morocco, 42:57

WOMEN
Lornah Kiplagat
Kenya, 50:06

MEN'S MASTERS
Peter Koech
Kenya, 47:16

WOMEN'S MASTERS
Jane Welzel
USA, 53:21

WHEELCHAIR MEN
Tony M. Nogueira
USA, 36:41

WHEELCHAIR WOMEN
Jessica Galli
USA, 52:06

Men's winner Khalid Khannouchi

Women's winner Lornah Kiplagat

Johanna Shaw of Rome, N.Y., crosses the finish line of the 1998 Utica Boilermaker Road Race wearing her bib and her father's honorary bib. Shaw and others wore T-shirts to remember her father, Ron Shaw, who had run in all Boilermaker races except the first one. The 1998 race would have been his 20th Boilermaker, but he died of cancer the April before the race. Johanna ran the previous three Boiler-makers with her father as he battled cancer. *Photo by Heather Martin*

Prefontaine, Alberto Salazar, Grete Waitz, Clarence DeMar, Bill Dellinger, Craig Virgin, Lynn Jennings, Fred Lebow and the 2002 inductees—John J. Kelley, Doris Brown Heritage, Bill Bowerman and Browning Ross.

Just about every sport imaginable had its own Hall of Fame before distance running came up with one. Race announcer Stewart said there was a reason for that—it was a cult sport before the boom of the 1970s. "In my mind, a Hall of Fame legitimizes a sport. Up until the 1970s, runners were largely marginal eccentrics, a few hundred of whom ran the Boston Marathon each year," he said.

"All that has changed in the last thirty years. Now we have the National Distance Running Hall of Fame to celebrate the history, the traditions and the memorabilia that make up our running heritage. At the Hall, the runners of today can connect with the great runners of years gone by. And what could be a more appropriate site than in Utica where one of the country's great road races, the Boilermaker, has grown up as part of the sport's lore."

Switzer emphasized the suitability of Utica as a site for the Hall of Fame because of the Boilermaker's strong connection to the community. "If little Cooperstown can get on the world map, then Utica can capitalize by having a Hall of Fame. This can have an economic impact on the community."

Switzer, the first woman to run the Boston Marathon officially, also feels runners more than deserve a place were they can be honored. "They're as great as any sports heroes," she said. "I don't think anyone works harder than runners. These people are great, great heroes."

And the Hall of Fame gives running—which Switzer said is the biggest

Ondoro Osoro (28) splashes himself with a cup of water. Khalid Khannouchi later came from behind to win the race. *Photo by Nancy L. Ford*

participation sport in the United States—a headquarters. "It validates the sport for people who do it, and educates those who don't."

Utica attorney John Petrone is co-director of the Hall of Fame with Boilermaker founder Earle Reed, and he is charged with developing support for the organization across the country. He has several ideas on how to do that, including using inductees to spread the word and enrolling other races as "charter" members in the Hall, lending support to the organization.

"The idea is to promote and preserve the sport of distance running," Petrone said. "I think it is important to educate people on the history of the sport, which goes all the way back to the ancient Greeks, and to educate people on health and fitness."

The Hall of Fame's connection to many of the legendary names of the sport and growing alliances with some of the most prestigious races in the nation—including the Boston, New York and Chicago Marathons—have helped make it known among the road-racing elite.

"I think the support we've gotten has become outstanding," Petrone said. "We've got a Who's Who of running involved in the Hall with the advisory board and our inductees. What we've got to do now is take those people who have gotten us there and to reach everyday runners."

Petrone and Earle Reed also hope to expand the Hall of Fame's reach by recruiting races as charter members that would support the Hall in exchange for cross-promotional opportunities, such as links to race Web sites.

In the five years since its founding, the Hall of Fame already has gained a great deal of exposure through its induction ceremonies, and the Boilermaker and its attendant activities and awards. The George Sheehan Media Award, presented during the Hall of Fame induction, and the Fred Lebow Award, presented during the New York City Marathon, are also sponsored by the Hall of Fame. The nominees for the Hall are announced at the annual New York Track Writers' luncheon, and the inductees are announced at a press conference sponsored by the Boston Athletic Association a few days before the Boston Marathon.

Khannouchi's 1998 Boilermaker victory was notable for several reasons. He ran down Ondoro Osoro late in the race and sprinted to a 42:57 finish to break a six-year Kenyan stranglehold on the men's

Wheelchair racers attack a hill while competing against each other and the clock during the race.
Photo by Elizabeth A. Mundschenk

open title. And Khannouchi, a Moroccan, would later bring reflected glory on the Boilermaker by setting a world record in the marathon by running a 2:05:42 time at Chicago the next year, then lowering it to 2:05:38 in London in 2002. He had already won Chicago in 1997, and would win again in 2000. He also became the center of a storm when he tried to become a United States citizen in time to qualify for the 2000 Olympics, but that didn't happen.

Khannouchi, who finished third in the 1996 race, said he had a plan entering the 1998 run.

"Stay with the group," he said. And he did. Osoro, the world 10-mile record-holder at the time, led from the first step.

He eventually built a 40-yard lead going down Champlin Avenue, after the 7th mile. Khannouchi and John Korir—he would become a Boilermaker champion in 1999 and 2001—quickly gained on Osoro, however, and caught him shortly before 8 miles. Khannouchi pulled ahead, led by 20 yards at 9 miles and streaked away to the finish.

"I'm a good kicker," he explained afterward. "I'm confident that when the race comes down to the end. I know I have a big chance to win."

Kenya's Lornah Kiplagat won the women's race for the second straight year in a second straight dramatic finish. Kiplagat, who had won the Los Angeles Marathon for the second consecutive time earlier in the year, outkicked country-woman Jane Omoro to win in 50:06, just a second and a few strides ahead.

It was the closest women's finish in the Boilermaker. Kiplagat had edged Hellen Kimaiyo-Kipkoskgei by 2 seconds—49:58 to 50:00—in the 1997 race.

The 1998 win came a little more than a week after Kiplagat finished second to Kimaiyo-Kipkoskgei in the 10-kilometer Peachtree Road Race. "I like 15K," she said. "It is more my race than 10K. I'm getting stronger as the race goes on. I like the distance, and I like the 15K most."

There apparently weren't many distances Kiplagat didn't like, because in succeeding years she did win Peachtree in Georgia a couple of times, as well as a variety of other international races of 4 miles and more.

Kenya's Peter Koech won the men's masters title, catching 1997 champion Martin Mondragon at 5 miles and going on to win in 47:16. Bill Rodgers, the 1983 men's open champion, ran in the 50-54 age group for the first time and won in 50:19, finishing fifty-second overall, the day after being inducted as a member of the first class of the National Distance Running Hall of Fame.

Mary Jane and Kevin Gagan of Albany, N.Y., cross the finish line hand-in-hand. *Photo by Elizabeth A. Mundschenk*

Alan Kuras, left, of Yorktown Heights, N.Y., lends a hand to Bob Jackson of Amawalk, N.Y., as they approach the finish line. *Photo by Nancy L. Ford*

Jane Welzel of Fort Collins, Colo., won the women's masters division in 53:21, 2 seconds better than the record set by former Olympic marathon champion Joan Benoit Samuelson, another member of the Hall of Fame's inaugural class.

The men's wheelchair race was the most dramatic ever, with Tony Nogueira of Glen Ridge, N.J., crossing the finish line a fraction of a second ahead of nineteen-year-old Josh Brunies of Hammond, La., with a time of 36:41. Nogueira also had won in 1996. Jessica Galli, fourteen, of Belle Mead, N.J., won the women's race for the second straight year, finishing in 52:06.

Ilion, N.Y., native Chris Getman, who recently had moved to Pennsylvania, was the top men's local finisher, running 48:29 for fortieth overall. Chris Sisting of Holland Patent, N.Y., ran 54:24 to repeat as the top local woman.

Dave Katz, of Finish Line Road Race Technicians, says that magical things still do happen in addition to collecting and accounting for accurate finish-line times. Katz said his biggest single thrill at the 1998 Boilermaker came when ten-year-old wheelchair racer Travis Quinnville of New Haven, Vt., was trying to complete the race and win a new racing chair.

The finish-line crew had already packed up its gear when Katz learned that Quinnville was still out on the course after more than four hours. Katz had the finish line quickly reassembled as word spread to the post-race party behind the F.X. Matt Brewery and hundreds and hundreds of runners returned to the finish-line area.

"I rode my bike to the top of the hill and told him there were all these people waiting down there just for him," Katz said.

Quinnville, accompanied by his mother, Tina, plus medical personnel, other wheelchair racers, police and security, struggled down Court Street as sirens whined and lights flashed. The crowd of more than a thousand roared as he hit the finish line.

YMCA massage therapist Kathy Mazur, left, works on Boilermaker runner Regina Epp's feet during the Health & Fitness Expo at the Masonic Home on July 10, 1998, in Utica, N.Y. Epp was running in her 12th Boilermaker.
Photo by Heather Martin

"It was the loudest cheer," Katz recalled. "I've never heard a sound like that. It was one of the greatest moments of my life."

The number of Boilermaker entries declined—to 8,629 from 9,458 the year before—but that was attributed to the 1997 race being the twentieth annual. In fact, the entry numbers grew the next few years, heading for an all-time high in the 25th annual race in 2002. A total of 7,340 finished the race in 1998.

Hall of Fame Has Local and National Leadership

John Petrone, a Utica attorney, and Earle Reed, founder of the Utica Boilermaker Road Race, are co-directors of the National Distance Running Hall of Fame.

Anyone can nominate someone to the Hall of Fame, and nominees are voted on by past inductees, members of the Mohawk Valley running community and members of the Hall's advisory board.

Petrone and Reed head the local contingent, which includes Don Bravemen of the Syracuse University School of Law, Dr. Mark Slavin, Boilermaker director Bob Ingalls, assistant director Dave Reichert, Joe Kelly, Dick Mattia, Jim Simpson and Jim Stasaitis.

The board, which meets once a year, is made up of distinguished members of the national running industry. They are Henley Gabeau, retired president of the Road Runners Club of America; George Hirsch, publisher of *Runners World* magazine; Don Kardong of the Road Runners Club of America; Carol Lasseter Rice, publisher of *Running Times* magazine; Craig Masback, CEO of USA Track & Field; Guy Morse, executive director of the Boston Athletic Association; Carey Pinkowski, executive director of the Chicago Marathon; Phil Stewart of Road Race Managment; Larry Rawson of ESPN; Allan Steinfeld, president of the Road Race Management; Linda K. Peterson, chairman of the board of the Susan G. Komen Breast Cancer Foundation; and Julia Emmons, director of the Atlanta (Ga.) Peachtree Road Race and president of the Atlanta Track Club.

1999

Youths Step Up

Catherine Ndereba already had won one Boilermaker. She won her second in the July 11, 1999, race—the first of a string of three in a row, and a course record as well.

John Korir, like Ndereba a Kenyan—no surprise there—won the first of his two titles.

The masters runners did well, too. New York State native John Tuttle took advantage of the 60° weather to streak to a course record in winning the men's title, and the irrepressible Diane Legare of Montreal won the women's crown for the second time.

And every one of the 7,376 finishers—8,689 entered—got to see their exact times as the Boilermaker used ChampionshipChip timing devices for the first time.

The day before, 1,500 youngsters participated in the Boilermaker's annual Youth Run, an incredibly successful spin-off of the race that had been inaugurated in 1989. Khalid Khannouchi, the 1998 Boilermaker champion who was injured and couldn't defend his title and who would set a world record (2:05:42) in the Chicago Marathon later that year, ran with them on the day before the big race.

Linda Beha, then the coordinator of the Youth Run, was taken by surprise by Khannouchi. "We didn't know he was going to be here," she said after the race. "It was great. That was a first for us to have one of the top runners in the Boilermaker run with the kids."

If Khannouchi made the kids and organizers happy, he also seemed to thoroughly enjoy himself, as well. "It was a lot of fun," he said after the race. "I don't get to enjoy running while I'm competing. I think it's our job, our responsibility to show the children the right way and support them in their races."

Khannouchi's participation led to other famous runners joining in the next year. Bill Rodgers, the four-time Boston Marathon and New York Marathon winner who won the Boilermaker in 1983, ran with the youngsters, along with 1972 Olympic marathon gold medalist Frank Shorter, three-time New York Marathon and one-time Boston Marathon champion Alberto Salazar and pioneer marathoner Nancy Kuscsik. All are members of the National Distance Running Hall of Fame.

"After watching Khannouchi last year, I thought it would be a good idea," Rodgers said. "I tried to get ahead of them and give them a pace."

In 2001, Craig Virgin, who was inducted into the Hall of Fame that weekend, did the same, as did Grete Waitz.

"That was the most amazing thing, to see those Hall of Fame runners run with the kids," said Terri Cannarelli, who now directs the race and has a staff of hundreds of volunteers. "Now, we're not going to let them not do it."

There were about 1,725 runners in the 2001 Youth Run, and there was a limit of 2,000 for the 25th Boilermaker. The first run was held July 9, 1989, the same day as the 12th annual Boilermaker. About two hundred children under the age of ten ran a quarter mile down to the Boilermaker finish line. The next year, there were three hundred seventy-five runners and twenty-four volunteers.

The Utica National Insurance Group has been the sole sponsor since the beginning. Bob Slitz of Utica National, Cindy LaFountain and Patti LaFountain

1999 HIGHLIGHTS

MEN
John Korir
Kenya, 43:00

WOMEN
Catherine Ndereba
Kenya, 48:52

MEN'S MASTERS
John Tuttle
USA, 46:17

WOMEN'S MASTERS
Diane Legare
Canada, 55:48

WHEELCHAIR MEN
Krige Schabort
USA, 33:35

WHEELCHAIR WOMEN
Laurie Stephens
USA 46:57

Men's winner John Korir

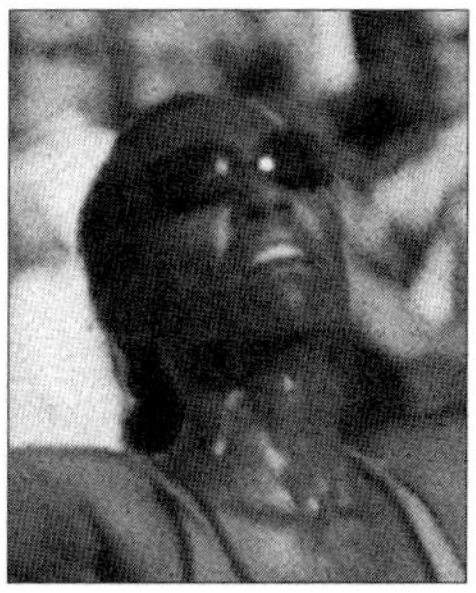

Women's winner Catherine Ndereba

coordinated the race in its early years. Beha headed the effort for several years, and Cannarelli, who had been Beha's assistant, took over in 2001. "I started as a volunteer," Cannarelli said. "I got my son involved when he was very young. I enjoyed seeing the socialization and health benefit from it.

"It definitely fueled my interest in running."

—Joe Hernon, now a 16-year-old from New Hartford, N.Y., on the Youth Run

"We [she and Beha, a colleague at Utica National] worked great as a team. She decided to step down. I just love it," she said. "It's a huge event in the community. It's the biggest children's event in the community all year long. I love putting it together and seeing the kids being so happy."

The Youth Run is now held the day before the Boilermaker in conjunction with the Health & Fitness Expo at the Masonic Home in Utica, N.Y. Children from age four to twelve run distances from a quarter mile to a mile. It's a non-competitive event, and all runners receive a T-shirt, goody bag and refreshments, and all their names are published in the *Observer-Dispatch*.

One of the objects of the Youth Run is to prepare youngsters to someday run the Boilermaker, and many Youth Run veterans do graduate to the big race.

Joe Hernon, now a sixteen-year-old from New Hartford, N.Y., who ran his third Boilermaker in the 25th annual race, is one of them. "I ran every year I could," he said. "It was a goal to move up to the Boilermaker. It definitely fueled my interest in running."

Hernon, a member of the New Hartford cross-country team, is a member of a "Youth Run family." His parents, Mary and Marty, aren't runners but are veteran volunteers. His brother, Mike, fourteen, is a former Youth Run participant, and his sisters Amanda, twelve; Lizzy, ten; and Rachel, six, take part each year.

The ChampionChips, which were sponsored by PAR Technology of New Hartford, proved to be a big plus, with almost all runners approving of them. The devices, first used in a sanctioned race in 1993 in the Netherlands, use computer technology to record when a runner crosses the starting line and then crosses the finish line. They provide an accurate elapsed time. In the past, runners in the back of the starting pack took as long as five and a half minutes to reach the start.

"You didn't have to wait in line, and you didn't have to push and shove to get into position," said Christina Brown of Clinton, N.Y., after the race.

"People were actually having fun at the start, versus trying to nudge each other," said Joe Kelly, veteran Boilermaker race official and runner.

The day before the race, the National

Daniel Mullen of Utica, N.Y., grimaces as he nears the finish line. *Photo by Elizabeth A. Mundschenk*

Distance Running Hall of Fame held its second annual induction. Johnny Kelley, who won the Boston Marathon twice and ran it sixty-one times altogether, couldn't be there to be honored, but he made the occasion memorable with his video tape-recorded version of "Young at Heart," sung with great style and verve.

Olympic heroes Francie Larrieu Smith and Billy Mills, and women's marathon pioneer Nancy Kuscsik also were inducted into the Hall of Fame that day.

From left, Lisa Hauck, Cory Fenton and Christopher Davis, all of New Hartford, N.Y., finish the race. *Photo by Elizabeth A. Mundschenk*

Runner Laura Luley (facing camera) shares a big hug with her friend Amanda Gomolka after the race. *Photo by Bradford S. Luppino*

Virginia Miller of Oneida, N.Y., celebrates as she crosses the finish line. *Photo by Elizabeth A. Mundschenk*

"It's a big thing in my life," said Kelley, who would soon turn ninety-two. "It brought me back to life, so to speak. It pleases me very much. I haven't been forgotten."

Both the men's and women's open races continued to attract some of the best runners in the world, continuing a string of very strong Boilermakers. In fact, the race was ranked the most competitive 15-kilometer race for five of the six years from 1996 through 2001 by Ken Young of the Analytical Distance Runner, and this one had fields as deep as any.

In 1999, eighty-one-year-old Elizabeth Hopsicker, of New Hartford, N.Y., cheers on her grandson, Fred Latus III of Whitesboro, N.Y., from her spot along Champlin Avenue. *Photo by Elizabeth A. Mundschenk*

Ndereba's victory came in her first Boilermaker after taking two years off following her 1996 win in Utica. Part of that layoff was used to take care of her daughter, Jane, who was born in 1997.

Ndereba outran two-time defending champion Lornah Kiplagat over the last 3 kilometers on the way to a course record of 48:52. Low humidity and a race-time temperature of 60º helped her do it. "Yes, I wanted to set a record," she said. "The conditions were very good."

Kiplagat (49:08), Margaret Okayo (49:09) and Jane Omoro (49:19) all bettered Kiplagat's 1997 record of 49:58.

"In the third mile, I tried to push it, then Lornah ran with me to 10K," Ndereba said. "Then I took the lead all the way to the finish."

Ndereba would win the next two Boilermakers as well, and also cover herself in glory by winning the Boston Marathon in 2000 and 2001 and setting a world record (2:18:47) in the 2001 LaSalle Bank Chicago Marathon. The 4-foot-11-inch, 86-pound Okayo—Ndereba is 5 feet 3 inches tall and weighs 98 pounds—would earn her own full measure of fame by outrunning Ndereba at Boston in a course record time (2:20:43) in 2002.

Korir used a strong finishing kick to best fellow Kenyan David Makori for the men's open title, 43:00 to 43:06. "It feels great," Korir said afterward. "It was nice and cool today."

Tuttle, a former Olympic marathoner who was born and raised in Alfred, N.Y., before going on to star at Auburn University, set a record in the men's masters race in 46:17, a half-minute better than the mark set by Martin Mondragon in 1997. Mondragon finished second this time around.

"I didn't know what the record was," said Tuttle, a teacher and coach in Douglaston, Ga., who had won the masters division at Atlanta's Peachtree Road Race in Georgia a few days before. "I was just looking to beat Mondragon."

Legare, forty-eight, finished in 55:48, 10 seconds ahead of Patti Ford of Lafayette, N.Y., to win her second Boilermaker masters title. The effervescent Legare said

John Korir of Kenya is all alone after pulling away from the lead pack of runners in 1999. Korir went on to win the 15-kilometer race. *Photo by Nancy L. Ford*

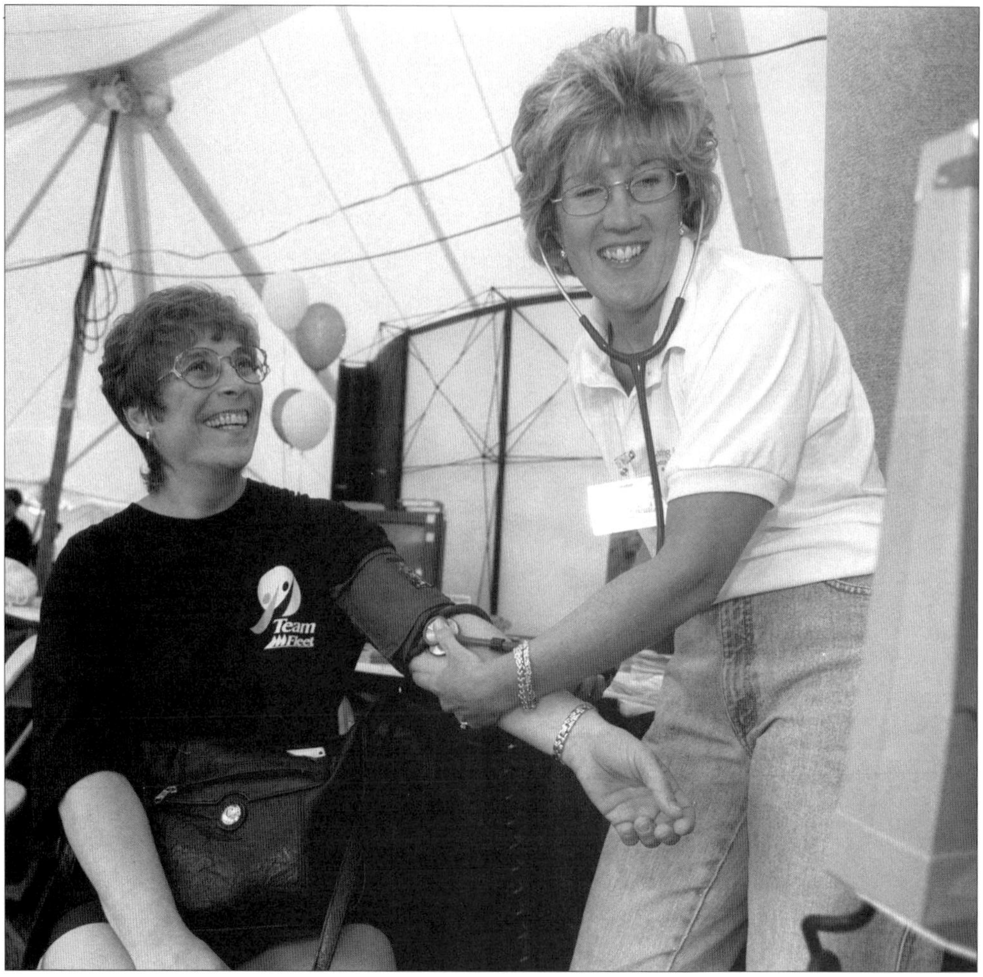

Sharon Costello, left, of Schuyler, N.Y., has her blood pressure checked by Mary Beth Dowling, R.N., during the Boilermaker Health & Fitness Expo at the Masonic Home in Utica on Friday, July 9, 1999. *Photo by Bradford S. Luppino*

she got a big push near the end of the race. "At the end, a Canadian runner passed me," she said. "I thought, 'I have to rush. He is sixty-six years old.'"

Legare, one of the many international runners who find the Boilermaker fun and exciting, praised the large and enthusiastic crowds along the course. "The crowd gives me some wings," she said in her not always precise but extremely heartfelt English. "It is amazing. The people participate. I mark it down on my calendar. It is my event of the year."

Ilion, N.Y., native Chris Getman was the top local men's open finisher, finishing thirty-fourth overall in 48:46. Two local masters runners did well, too. Dan Cohen was third in the 60-69 age group in 1:03:57 and Howard Rubin was third in the 70-90 age group in 1:12:42.

Chris Sisting of Marcy, N.Y., was the top local women for the third consecutive year, finishing in 57:58.

Krige Shabort of Cedartown, Ga., won the men's wheelchair race in 33:35, and fifteen-year-old Laurie J. Stephens of Wenham, Mass., won the women's wheelchair race in 46:57.

Former Olympic marathoner Dick Buerkle won the 50-59 men's masters race in 49:48.

2000

Local Runners in the Spotlight

New Hartford, N.Y.'s Dave Butler looks forward to the Utica Boilermaker Road Race more than he does to Christmas. "It's the best party day of the year," he said. "And talking to different people from out of town and out of state, to hear the positive things they say about something in our area, makes me want to be a part of that."

Countless others feel the same.

So, as Catherine Ndereba continued to build her reputation with another victory on July 9 and Reuben Cheruiyot outfought former two-time champion Joseph Kimani to earn the men's title, thousands and thousands of recreational runners were out there pounding the pavement in the 2000 race. Some rolled to impressive times, but the bulk of them simply and relentlessly churned out the miles to the best of their ability, getting the job done in something more than an hour or maybe 90 minutes or even 130, and having a great time.

The 23rd annual race was dedicated to Jim Morgan, the late Oneida County (N.Y.) Family Court judge who had run each of the first twenty-one Boilermakers. Morgan, one of those "citizen runners," died in September 1999 after a battle with pancreatic and liver cancer.

The race was also the last as director for founder Earle Reed, with Bob Ingalls scheduled to take over in 2001. Reed, however, remained intimately connected to the race and with the National Distance Running Hall of Fame, which he began to serve as co-director with Utica, N.Y., attorney John Petrone.

For all the attention paid to the incredibly talented elite runners from around the world, the widening spotlight on the Hall of Fame and the local renown for

2000 HIGHLIGHTS

MEN
Reuben Cheruiyot
Kenya, 43:07

WOMEN
Catherine Ndereba
Kenya, 48:47

MEN'S MASTERS
Andrew Masai
Kenya, 44:56
(course and race record)

WOMEN'S MASTERS
Marina Belyaeva
Russia, 53:47

WHEELCHAIR MEN
Saul Mendoza
USA 32:40
(course record)

WHEELCHAIR WOMEN
Laurie Stephens
USA 46:26
(course record)

More than 9,000 runners get started along the 15K course of the 2000 Utica Boilermaker Road Race.
Photo by Nancy L. Ford

**Men's winner
Reuben Cheruiyot**

**Women's winner
Catherine Ndereba**

the best area runners, the Boilermaker has remained a people's race. A high percentage of the runners are everyday recreationists. Some of them are very good runners. Some are just determined. Some run nearly every year. Some have run but once.

Robert Moon of Boonville, N.Y., ran his only Boilermaker in 1997, when he was seventy. "At that point, I was trying to lose a little weight," he said. "I tried everything else. I started in April and I faithfully trained. Somebody told me if you could run 6 miles on any given day, you could do the Boilermaker, and that's the way it worked."

You'd have to put Moon in the determined category. His time was 2:18:25. "I'm not a runner," he said. "There were only twenty guys behind me."

Moon hasn't run a Boilermaker since because of a series of health problems, but hasn't given up the idea of running again.

Star-spangled Peter J. Haggerty of West Henrietta, N.Y., gestures toward Luane R. Davis, also of West Henrietta, as they approach the finish line. *Photo by Elizabeth A. Mundschenk*

Brian Lytwynec of Ilion, N.Y., ran only a couple of Boilermakers—he finished the 20th anniversary race in 1997 in 1:21:08—and probably never will run it again because of back surgery. The former Section III discus and shot put champion, who went on to compete in track and play football at the University of Pennsylvania, has some terrific memories of the race, however. "For me, the most fantastic part was the first 2 or 3 miles, when you're caught in that river of people, the momentum pulling you along," he said. "That's what I remember most about the Boilermaker."

Dan Cohen, on the other hand, has run nearly every race, and has won his age group a couple of times, including 2001, at age sixty-five. He began running in 1978, training for the first Boilermaker. "What's great about the Boilermaker is the crowd participation," said Cohen, a Utica attorney. "It's exciting to have people from the time you start till the time you finish calling your name, knowing who you are. It's invigorating, energizing. And the Boilermaker has great competition in the masters age groups."

You don't have to be from Central New York to love the Boilermaker. Rick Rumsey of South Glastonbury, Conn., ran the race for the first time in 1996, encouraged by fellow Hamilton College, Clinton, N.Y., alumni from the Mohawk Valley. "They told me it was the greatest race in the U.S. and that I had to come up and run it," he said. "I haven't missed a year since. At first I thought it was a chance to drink beer at 9 o'clock on a Sunday morning. It turned out to be a lot more than that."

Rumsey runs only one other race, the Manchester, Conn., Thanksgiving Run, which will celebrate its sixty-sixth birthday this year. A former Hamilton football player, he usually runs in the Boilermaker in the low 70-minute range and has done it in 1:09:00.

"To participate when the streets are lined with everybody in the city, either people helping put the race on or running in it themselves, I love that community spirit and participation," he said. "It's a feel-good thing. It's nice to see a com-

Michelle Waite (8674) rejoices as she crosses the finish line of the 2000 Utica Boilermaker Road Race hand-in-hand with fellow Ilion, N.Y., resident Angela Belmont. *Photo by Michael Doherty*

munity come together and I like the tradition of it."

Butler, a New Hartford town councilman, began running a couple of years before the Boilermaker was born and has failed to run the race only three times. "I missed in 1997 and I'll never forget the feeling I had watching it," he said. "I'll never not run it again. It's part of me, part of the community. I will run it as long as I'm physically able to and I'm in town. If it came down to where I couldn't run, I'd probably go away the day of the race."

Butler's sisters, Pat DelMedico and Carol Spinella, are or have been Boilermaker runners; so has his brother-in-law Dominic Spinella; niece and nephew Julie and Andy DelMedico; his daughter, Kim, and his son-in-law, Matt Lee. Running the race a few years ago with Kim was a thrill for him, and so has running with Kevin Martin and Tim Solan, his teammates on the New Hartford Fire Department Corporate Cup team.

Sandy D'Onofrio ran her fifteenth consecutive Boilermaker in 2002, although it isn't necessarily her favorite race. She isn't fast and doesn't like to run in the heat of summer, so she prefers America's Greatest Heart Run in Utica, which is held every February. She works out all year, however—"I run to eat"—she said, and the Boilermaker remains an important personal challenge. "I do enjoy myself, but I'm not about times and I'm not about competition," she said. "It's 'you're a year older, but you can still do it.'"

She said she also likes the ritual of it all. "For as many years as I've run it, I see the same people in the same spots [along the course]," she said. "The lady who always gives you ice. Or you're coming up to a spot and you know who is going to be there. That's a cool thing."

Ndereba's victory in the women's open race was not unexpected, and she easily defeated fellow Kenyan Hellen Kimaiyo-Kipkosgei, turning in a time of 48:47 to break her own record of 48:52

set the year before. Kimaiyo-Kipkosgei finished in 49:35, and no one else was even close, with Yuko Arimori of Japan third in 51:51.

That Ndereba was here at all for the 2000 race was perhaps a bit unexpected, however. In April, she had become the first Kenyan woman to win the Boston Marathon, earning $80,000. She followed that up with a second in the New York Mini Marathon in June, then returned to Africa.

Instead of staying home and enjoying the fruits of her labor, Ndereba returned to run in the United States. She came back for a couple of reasons. One, because she was not chosen in the marathon for Kenya's Olympic team and wanted to train to try to qualify in the 10,000 meters, and also because she simply liked the race.

She ran second at Atlanta, Georgia's Peachtree Road Race 10K on July 4, and then won the Boilermaker under cloudy skies that produced temperatures in the low 60s at race time. She earned the $5,000 top prize, plus another $1,000 bonus for setting another record. "I was not out to set a record today," she said afterward. "Due to the climate, I ended up being able to set the course record."

"I'm not about times and I'm not about competition."

—Sandy D'Onofrio, of the Mohawk Valley, on why she races

Ndereba and Kimaiyo-Kipkosgei started out running together. "But that first mile was 5:27," Ndereba said. "That was not the pace I wanted. I just tried to push the pace, keep up with the pace, and then I found myself running by myself."

Ndereba, obviously, was gratified she made the decision to come back to the United States to race.

"Yes, I came back here and I pray to God I come back next year and shatter my course record again," she said. "I love Utica. Everyone has got the spirit of everyone helping each other."

And, of course, she did come back in 2001 and did shatter her course record again, with an incredible time of 48:06. The time also buried the informal race record of 48:19 set by England's Jill Hunter in 1991, before the course was slightly reconfigured in 1997.

Cheruiyot came in as one of the favorites in a deep field.

Defending champion John Korir and former champions Lazarus Nyakeraka (1995) and Joseph Kimani (1996, 1997), along with South African stars Simon Bor, Abner Chipu and Gert Thys, were entered, as were David Makori, Peter Githuka and Joseph Kamau, all of whom had finished second in recent years.

Cheruiyot was having an especially hot season. Although he had finished third at Peachtree, he had won the Washington, D.C., Cherry Blossom 10-Mile—Kimani was second—in April and the Lilac Bloomsday in Spokane, Wash., the Arts Fest River Run in Evansville, Ind., and the Examiner Bay to Breakers in San Francisco in May.

Kimani, who set the course record of 42:54 in 1997 and the race record of 42:40 in 1996, led through the 9th mile, but Cheruiyot charged past him in the last 200 meters to finish in 43:07. "I wanted to outkick Kimani," Cheruiyot said. "I wasn't sure I could do it."

Kimani knew differently, which is why he tried to put some distance between himself and Cheruiyot, Nyakeraka and Ethiopia's Alene Emere as the race neared the stretch. Nyakeraka and Emere began to fall back after 8 miles, and then Cheruiyot slid into Kimani's tracks.

Kimani wanted desperately to lose his rival, but couldn't do it and didn't have enough left for a strong kick. "I was tired with 400 meters to go," he said. "I knew he was behind me. I knew he would win. I was tired. He was relaxed."

Cheruiyot did take off, but Kimani did hang with him pretty well, finishing 3 seconds back, in 43:10.

The $5,000 prize pushed Cheruiyot's winnings for the year to about $40,000.

The men's masters race was interesting in large part because Andrew Masai's victory in a record time of 44:56 signaled

Chuck Lester of Ilion, N.Y., gives really high fives to Boilermaker runners as they pass by him along Champlin Avenue in Yorkville, N.Y. It was Lester's sixth year encouraging the runners from his stilts. *Photo by Elizabeth A. Mundschenk*

Candace M. Zywiak of Marcy, N.Y., cools off with a cup of water offered by a volunteer along Champlin Avenue in Yorkville, N.Y., during the race.
Photo by Elizabeth A. Mundschenk

a new era in the forty-plus category. A number of Kenyan runners were just hitting that age, and everyone knew what that meant. John Tuttle sure did. He had set the record of 46:17 in 1999, when he won sixteen races and was ranked as the top masters runner in the world.

"The Kenyans are here, and I'll never get away from them," said Tuttle, who finished fourth in the 2000 race in 46:59. "I'm a realist. Now I realize, shoot, I'm not that great. But I had my time in the sun. You only have a small window, so you race like crazy."

Wilson Waigwa was the first Kenyan to win a Boilermaker masters title, in 1989, and Peter Koech won in 1998. Masai, who had just turned forty and would win again in 2001 and 2002, made it obvious that the Kenyans would continue to be threats. "In Kenya, I am training with my friends, the young Kenyans," he said. "And I stay behind them."

That's how he ran the Boilermaker. He stayed with the lead pack of twenty-somethings for 7 miles before dropping back, but not way back. He was nineteenth overall. "I didn't believe I got down to 44 minutes," he said after the race. "I didn't plan for that at this age."

Simon Karori of Kenya was a distant second in 46:00, with Graeme Fell of British Columbia third in 46:22.

Russia's Marina Belyaeva won the women's masters in 53:47, outdueling Sabrina Robinson of Tempe, Ariz., (54:19) and the 1999 champion, Diane Legare of Montreal (55:12). Because of a very thin women's open field, that trio enjoyed a good cash bonus. Belyaeva, Robinson and Legare picked up $1,000, $500 and $300, respectively, for finishing first, second and third in the masters division and $600, $300 and $200, respectively, for finishing seventh, ninth and tenth in the open division.

Ilion, N.Y., native Chris Getman was the top local men's finisher, running 48:06 to take thirty-eighth place overall. The time was a personal best and he credited his Syracuse (N.Y.) Chargers Track Club teammate, Mike Melfi, with helping him run it.

Melfi, a Henninger (Syracuse, N.Y.) High School graduate, ran 47:35, thirty-fourth overall.

"He is the guy who really pushed me," Getman said. "I was with him for 5 miles, and then he really started to roll. He's a great guy to race with."

Susan Sivers-Corrigan was the top local woman in a time of 1:02:01. Farrell Burns, formerly of Clinton, N.Y., and a former All-American at Colby College in Waterville, Maine, had the top time of any woman with a local connection, 58:58. Numerous local women ran well, including Christine Campbell of Waterville, N.Y., (1:02:24) and her sister, Joanne (1:03:23); Karen Vanderwood of Utica, (1:03:24); Ingrid Otto-Jones of Utica, (1:04:09); and Christina Raulli of Rome, N.Y., (1:04:14).

Saul Mendoza of Snellville, Ga., rocketed to the men's wheelchair title in a record time of 32:40, and Laurie Stephens of Wenham, Mass., won the women's championship for the second consecutive time, finishing in 46:26.

The evening before the race, the National Distance Running Hall of Fame held its third annual induction at the Stanley Performing Arts Center. Marathon greats Grete Waitz and Alberto Salazar joined the Hall, along with the late Steve Prefontaine and the late Clarence DeMar.

The race drew 9,040 runners, and 7,889 finished—a record, but one that would last only a year.

2001

Woman's Winner Extends Her Rule

She already was known as Catherine the Great. In 2001, however, Kenya's Catherine Ndereba extended her rule over the road-racing world as few runners ever had, winning fourteen times and collecting hundreds of thousands of dollars in prize money.

Battling countrywoman Esther Kiplagat and South Africa's Elana Meyer, Ndereba won her third consecutive Utica Boilermaker Road Race on July 8, 2001, with her third consecutive record time, a 48:06 that not only shattered her previous best of 48:47 but also broke the all-time race record of 48:19. England's Jill Hunter had set that mark in 1991, before the course was slightly reconfigured in 1997, and it had been regarded by many as the best performance in Boilermaker history by a woman or a man.

Kenya's John Korir earned his second Boilermaker men's open title—he also won in 1999—outkicking South Africa's Shadrack Hoff by a scant second, 42:57 to 42:58.

The men's race was unusual because of the large number of runners who stayed in contention through Valley View Golf Course, up the long incline of Burrstone Road and down the fast mile along Champlin Avenue. Alene Emere of Ethiopia was another second behind Hoff in

2001 HIGHLIGHTS

MEN
John Korir
Kenya, 42:57

WOMEN
Catherine Ndereba
Kenya, 48:06
(course and race record)

MEN'S MASTERS
Andrew Masai
Kenya, 45:13

WOMEN'S MASTERS
Elena Fidatov
Romania, 53:18

WHEELCHAIR MEN
Saul Mendoza
USA 33:30

WHEELCHAIR WOMEN
Jessica Galli
USA, 47:20

High school stand-out Alan Webb walks with running legend Bill Rodgers after they completed the Boilermaker in Utica, N.Y., on Sunday, July 8, 2001. *Photo by Michael Doherty*

Women's winner Catherine Ndereba

April Coughlin, of New Paltz, N.Y., celebrates at the finish line at the 2001 race. She was the second female to finish in the wheelchair division. *Photo by Michael Doherty*

42:59, with Gilbert Koech, Gilbert Okari, David Makori and 1995 champion Lazarus Nyakeraka all hitting the line in 43:07 or better, the closest mass finish ever. Evans Rutto and Eliud Lagata of Kenya and Tekeste Kebede of Ethiopia all were 43:17 or better.

Andrew Masai of Kenya, who set a men's masters record of 44:56 in 2000, won that division again in 45:13. Elena Fidatov of Romania set a women's masters course record of 53:18, and Saul Mendoza (a record 33:30) and Jessica Galli (47:20) won the wheelchair divisions.

Boilermaker men's winner John Korir (2) of Kenya runs neck-and-neck with second-place finisher Shadrack Hoff (16) of South Africa and third-place finisher Alene Emere (25) of Ethiopia on Burrstone Road near the 6-mile mark. *Photo by Darren Phillips*

Utica (N.Y.) Fire Department EMTs Doug Hauge, left, and Mike Belmont, right, tend to a runner who collasped on Champlin Avenue.
Photo by Nancy L. Ford

The Utica, N.Y., victory was just one in a sensational year for Ndereba, who turned twenty-nine just two weeks after the race, on July 21.

Ndereba, who won the Boston Marathon a second straight time in April, won those fourteen races during the year and earned $365,000 in prize money. Later, on October 7, she wrote her name boldly into the history books when she set a world record of 2:18:47 in winning the LaSalle Bank Chicago Marathon.

The success made Ndereba much in demand, and led to her decision not to return to Utica to run for a fourth consecutive championship in the 25th annual race in 2002. She and agent Lisa Buster asked for appearance money for racing. "We feel it is warranted," Buster said—but the Boilermaker stood by its policy of not paying more than expenses.

Still, 2001 provided a hard-to-believe string of accomplishments for the 5-foot-3-inch, 98-pound Ndereba, although she barely takes credit for them. Her explanation for her sensational, all-but-unprecedented season? "Well, I think I know God is on my side, because without Him I can't do it," said Ndereba, who is very serious about her Presbyterian faith, a few days before finishing second to countrywoman Margaret Okayo in the 2002 Boston Marathon. "It is just by the power of the Holy Spirit."

Ndereba grew up in the village of Nyeri, about one hundred miles from Nairobi. Although athletic competition by women was frowned on there, her father supported her and she began running in American road races in 1995. She won her first Boilermaker in 1996, then took two seasons off after giving birth to her daughter, Jane, in 1997. "I think she is going to be a runner," she said of her daughter. "She says she wants to be a doctor."

Ndereba had been pointing toward a world record on Chicago's fast course since winning in 2:21:33 there in 2000. And she knew she could get it done after Japan's Naoko Takahashi broke the 2:20 barrier with a 2:19:46 in the Berlin Marathon just a week before the 2001 Chicago race.

Ndereba started Chicago slowly, and found herself well behind a record pace 10 miles into the race. Once she realized that, she took off, running the 11th mile in 5:07:8. She was especially strong in the final half, covering the half marathon distance in 1:08:33, an average of 5:13:7 per mile.

The fourteen victories and the world record made Ndereba as much or more of

The lead pack of runners makes its way through the Valley View Golf Course along the Boilermaker route. *Photo by Elizabeth A. Mundschenk*

a heroine in her country as Tegla Loroupe, Kenya's female road-racing pioneer. At least, everyone knows her name.

"People don't really recognize her on the street," Buster said. "She wears dresses, not running clothes; she wears her hair down, not back."

That's a good thing, Ndereba said. "I just come and go as always," she said.

Her great wealth by Kenyan standards is shared with her extended family and others she cares about, especially young girls who want to be competitive runners. "I don't care about the money," she said in her clipped, lightly accented English. "I just live as Catherine. I count it as a blessing from God."

"I count it as a blessing from God."

—Kenya's Catherine Ndereba, on her knack for winning

Ndereba's training for Utica, Chicago and all her races in 2001 was much the same as always. She was up at 5:30 A.M. to run for two hours, back home for breakfast, and out for a jog at about 10 A.M. She ran between one hundred and one hundred ten miles a week.

Her strategy regarding opponents or the course—in any race? "I don't think about anything," she said. "I just think about the race."

Ndereba and Meyer, the world-record holder for 15K (46:57), ran shoulder-to-shoulder for much of the 2001 Boilermaker until Ndereba pulled away in the last mile. Esther Kiplagat was along for the ride, too. Meyer, a silver medal winner in the 1992 Olympics at 10,000 meters, finished 5 seconds behind Ndereba in 48:11—also under Hunter's blazing 1991 time—and Kiplagat was third in 48:25.

"It could've been better if I'd won, but we had fantastic conditions and a good course and a good community," Meyer said.

Ndereba said Meyer helped push her through the race and Buster said the record might not have been broken if Meyer had not been in the field. "Elana pushed her along," she said. "It's always her goal to beat her best time, but Elana really drove her to break Jill Hunter's record."

Ndereba was happy to get the record, but just as happy to run a personal best. And Meyer was extremely gracious in finishing second. "She's a great athlete, having a fantastic year," she said. "She's the best marathon runner in the world, definitely No. 1 at the moment. I was beaten by a great athlete."

Korir had beaten fellow Kenyan David Makori by 6 seconds in winning his first Boilermaker title in 1999, surging to the lead in the last mile and a half.

The 2001 race was quite different. Korir, who had won the Cherry Blossom 10-Mile in Washington, D.C., in April and Atlanta's Peachtree Road Race 10K on July 4, had to run in a pack of a dozen runners for more than 8 miles, and seven runners were still in contention at the 9-mile mark.

That was something new for the Boilermaker. Normally, just two or three runners are still in the hunt at that point.

Then, with just over a quarter mile to go, Korir and Hoff broke away, streaking down Court Street with the crowd cheering wildly. Korir got to the finish line first. "I knew I could outkick him," Korir said. "I was very confident."

Hoff had tried to sprint away from Korir at 9 miles, but couldn't do it. "He has a better kick, and he wanted me to kick first," said the South African Olympian. "Next time, I will be ready."

Chris Getman, originally from Ilion, N.Y., was the top men's runner with a local connection, finishing thirty-first in 47:18. Tom Smith of Whitesboro, N.Y., ran 52:07 to win the 45-49 age group for the third straight year. Clinton, N.Y.'s Hamilton College All-American Maggie Hanson, from Bowdoinham, Maine, the NCAA Division III indoor champion at 5,000 meters, was thirtieth in the women's open race in 58:47. Former Clinton (N.Y.) High School athlete Farrell Burns was thirty-second in 59:02.

The race continued to grow and improve. There were 9,317 entrants, the second most ever, and a record 8,181 finishers. The percentage of finishers was eighty-eight, matching the Boilermaker's all-time high.

The night before the race, the National Distance Running Hall of Fame inducted a foursome of standouts—University of Oregon cross-country and track coach Bill Dellinger, two-time world cross-country champion and Olympian Craig Virgin, three-time Olympian and three-time world cross-country runner Lynn Jennings and the late Fred Lebow, founder of the New York City Marathon.

The Hall of Fame also presented its inaugural Bill Bowerman Award to Jeff Johnson, former coach of the Nike Farm Team for post-collegiate runners, as the National Distance Running coach of the year, and presented the George Sheehan Media Award to Hamilton College graduate Dick Patrick, longtime track-and-field writer for *USA Today*.

The leaders head up Valley View Road during the Sunday race.
Photo by Elizabeth A. Mundschenk

Founder and former director of the Utica Boilermaker Road Race, Earle Reed, left, talks with present director Bob Ingalls near the finish line. *Photo by Michael Doherty*

Venketta Mannava of Utica, N.Y., leads a wave of runners with arms upraised as they neared the finish line in front of the F. X. Matt Brewery on Court Street. *Photo by Michael Doherty*

2002

Reaching the Quarter-Century Mark

There might never really be a consensus on whether the 25th Boilermaker on July 14 was the best ever. There have been a lot of very good ones—and it's a matter of opinion, anyway. Possibly the loudest and most raucous? Again, it can be argued.

But the biggest? There is no doubt of that. The Utica Boilermaker Road Race celebrated its 25th birthday with a massive showing of runners, fans, volunteers, and partyers and it all went off practically without a hitch as thousands of runners from around the Mohawk Valley, across New York State and the country—and from around the world—thundered through the streets of Utica, N.Y., on a bright, sunny day.

"Excellent," raved race founder Earle Reed. "With any big production, there always can be some fine tuning. There is nothing that can't be improved upon. Having said that, you can't lose sight of the big picture. We've had a rousing success changing people's lives for the better."

The Boilermaker hit new highs in any number of categories. There were 11,667 entrants, a record by more than two thousand runners. There were 9,797 finishers, the most ever by more than 1,600. There were thousands of fans cheering along the course in numbers impossible to estimate.

And there were at least 30,000 people, perhaps 35,000, singing and dancing and just having a great time at the massive post-race party in the back parking lot of the F.X. Matt Brewery.

"I couldn't see the back of the crowd," beamed Boilermaker race director Bob Ingalls, reporting on the view from the stage during the awards ceremony.

Still, the race wasn't all about big and loud. It simply lived up to its reputation as the best thing that happens in the Utica-Rome-Mohawk Valley area every year.

"This was by far the best and most meaningful Boilermaker," exulted Tom Rothstein, a runner from Springfield, Mass. "Twenty-five years. Good for you, Utica."

Kenya's Paul Kosgei, who made his American road-racing debut with a victory July 4 at the Peachtree Road Race 10K in Atlanta, Georgia, broke away from the field at the 7-mile mark and easily won the men's open race in a rather slow 43:22. Kosgei broke the tape held by Reed and Gov. George Pataki, the first New York chief executive ever to visit the race.

Pataki was impressed by the race itself and all the surrounding fanfare. "This is tremendous—the crowds, the runners," he said. "I've seen a lot of races, but nothing like this. This is clearly one of the great events in the country."

Constantina Dita, one of a number of Romanian runners beginning to make their marks in American road racing, won the women's open race in 48:29, defeating countrywoman Luminita Talpos by more than a minute (49:35). Andrew Masai of Kenya won the men's masters (40 and over) race for the third straight year, this time in 46:25.

Romania's Elena Fidatov turned in what might have been the best performance of the day, streaking to her second consecutive women's masters title in 52:01, taking 1:17 off the course record she set in 2001 and also erasing the race record of 52:03 run by Tatyana Pozdnyakova of the Ukraine in 1996, the year before the course was reconfigured.

2002 HIGHLIGHTS

MEN
Paul Kosgei
Kenya, 43:22

WOMEN
Constantina Dita
Romania, 48:29

MEN'S MASTERS
Andrew Masai
Kenya, 46:25

WOMEN'S MASTERS
Elena Fidatov
Romania, 52:01
(course and race record)

WHEELCHAIR MEN
Kamel B. Ayari
New Rochelle, 36:53

WHEELCHAIR WOMEN
April Coughlin
New Paltz, 50:53

Men's winner Paul Kosgei

Women's winner Constantina Dita

Kamel Ayari of New Rochelle, N.Y., won the men's wheelchair race in 36:53, with April Coughlin of New Paltz, N.Y., winning the women's division in 50:53.

As always, landmark 25th birthday or not, the Boilermaker remained as much a monumental party-reunion-fair-celebration as it is a race. It put a smile on everyone's face.

"Do you think they'll have the race next year?"

—Racing legend Bill Rodgers jesting after the 25th Boilermaker

"I thought it was great," said Maureen Levine Ruhm, who has run an unofficial ice station on Burrstone Road for the last dozen years. "The racers are so appreciative and the party afterward is wonderful. And we actually got the governor here! It must be an election year."

Ruhm and her friend Janine Valeriano started out bringing eight bags of ice to their location, which is on a long, gradual, particularly shadeless uphill stretch a little more than 6 miles into the race. This year, they used twenty-five bags of ice. They were assisted by Ruhm's mother, Mary Alice Levine, and Susan Filippone.

"My mouth is going the whole time," Ruhm said. "I make it a carnival atmosphere. 'Ice here, it's cold and it's free.' "

Levine said the 2002 race was about the same as all the others she's watched. "Other than it being the biggest race, I didn't see anything different," she said. "And the reason it wasn't any different is because it is always so well planned. It's always a good time. Actually, there was a difference. Many people had flags. Some carried them. Some had them on their running clothes. Spectators had them. There were a lot of American flags. We even had one on our ice station."

Patriotism was indeed a consistent theme in the race, with the events of September 11, 2001, still fresh in everyone's minds. That made the flyover by the F-16s from the 174th Fighter Wing of the New York Air National Guard in Syracuse particularly thrilling for every-

Boilermaker fans, including Paul Serafini (6171) of Worcester, Mass., cheer the band during the party after the 2002 race. *Photo by Nancy L. Ford*

Michael J. Geiss of Clayton, N.Y., makes his way through the Valley View Golf Course. *Photo by Elizabeth A. Mundschenk*

one. The four jets twice shot over the post-race crowd, sending up a tremendous roar of appreciation, as always.

The landmark race was special for many other reasons. Running legends Bill Rodgers and Frank Shorter made their annual appearances—Rodgers won $100 by finishing fourth in the masters 50-59 division with a 53:52—and Ric Rojas, who won the men's open title in the very first Boilermaker in 1978, also returned.

Rojas ran with his son, Rico, twenty, and they finished together in 1:25:47. Rojas won that first race in 45:38. He ran again in 1982, when he was fifth behind winner Jim O'Connell of Syracuse, N.Y. "It's great," Rojas said. "I was able to share this experience with Rico. It's like a time capsule for him. He got to meet people like Bill Rodgers."

The race also was special for those have run every one since 1978. There are twenty such runners left, since Sam Gratch, seventy-seven, was unable to continue his streak following a stroke and then an accident in which he was hit by a car and knocked off his bike, breaking his elbow.

Richard Watkajtys, one of the "perennial runners," said the festivities surrounding the 25th running were what made the day so special. "The whole weekend was fabulous," he said. "It was like standing in the dugout of Yankee Stadium, talking to the big stars—Bill Rodgers, Frank Shorter and Amby Burfoot.

"I don't know if I have twenty-five more in me. Like Butch Custodero [another perennial] said, 'We have as many more as God gives us—no more, no less.' That's a good quote."

The 25th annual Boilermaker didn't quite live up to its reputation for heat and humidity. It was a relatively comfortable 68° at race time, but it did climb to 77° by 10 A.M. and many runners did complain. More than a dozen runners were taken to hospitals and two were admitted, but there were no serious injuries.

The elite runners weren't bothered by much of anything, of course.

Kosgei was just too much for the men's field, including defending champion John Korir, who also won in 1999. Local favorite Jerry Lawson, the former Mohawk Valley Community College star and former Chicago Marathon American record holder, led for nearly the first 3 miles of the race, with a pack of about two dozen Africans 75 yards behind him.

"There is no way those guys should be behind me," said Lawson, who said he was merely trying to run his own pace. "I had no idea what was going on."

A slow first couple of miles, for one thing. Lawson ran a glacial 9:45 for 2 miles and the Africans were even slower. Kosgei and Korir spent the time sizing each other up, each trying to figure the other's strategy. Perhaps a half dozen runners led for short stretches over the first 10 kilometers, and there was still at pack of ten runners when they hit the turn onto Champlin Avenue and headed for the 7-mile marker near the entrance to Utica College.

That's when the leaders strung out single file, and when Kosgei ran away. "I didn't see anybody who wanted to attack it," he said. "I started to pull away and nobody came with me."

Within a couple of minutes Kosgei built a lead of 75 yards, and no one was able to challenge. He finished in 43:22, far off the course record of 42:54 set by Joseph Kimani in 1997. Korir was second in 43:31, followed by Hendrick Ramaala (43:34), Tom Nyariki (43:35) and Gilbert Koech (43:37).

Dita ran her race unchallenged. The only thing that bothered her were the downhills, which might have cost her shot at Catherine Ndereba's course and race record of 48:06. "After about 10K, there was a downhill part," she said. "I don't like the downhill. I don't like it at all. I have problems with my leg, and the downhill bothers it." Otherwise, she had no problems at all.

Masai became the first three-time men's masters winner—the first three-time men's winner in either of the top two divisions—by holding off Russia's Gennady Temnikov, 46:25 to 46:32.

Fidatov flew to her victory, earning the masters prize of $1,000, plus an additional $200 for finishing ninth overall in the women's division. "I know the course, I know that we have the hill [Steele Hill Road] and because I trained in Boulder [Colo.] before and ran many hills, today that was good for me," she said.

As always, local runners played a key role in the race.

Joanne Campbell of Waterville, N.Y., and Colgate University in Hamilton, N.Y., was the top local female runner, finishing thirty-second in 1:00:35. Former Hamilton College (Clinton, N.Y.) star Maggie Hanson was thirty-fourth in 1:00:58; former Vernon Center, N.Y., resident Heidi Gerken was forty-fourth in 1:01:37; Anita Moller of Whitesboro, N.Y., was forty-fifth in 1:01:40; Jackie Kosakowski of Sauquoit, N.Y., was forty-eighth in 1:02:07; Kelly Dworak of New Hartford, N.Y., finished in 1:02:33.

Matt Spring of Holland Patent, N.Y., and Manahattan College was the top local male runner, placing forty-seventh in 50:01, his best finish. Ithaca's Chris Getman, an Ilion, N.Y., native, had the best time of anyone with a local connection, finishing thirty-eighth in 47:20. Former Providence College star Tom Smith of Whitesboro won the 45-59 age group for the fourth consecutive year and finished eighty-fifth overall in 52:53.

In the end, the 2002 Boilermaker bore little resemblance to its predecessor of twenty-five years before. The budget was a thousand times the original—$746,057 as opposed to $750, with close to something like a third of that going to support the National Distance Running Hall of Fame—the field had grown from 930 to more than ten times that, and the attendant hoopla of golf tournaments, training runs, walks, the Expo and the rest had all but engulfed the community.

And, with few exceptions, everyone continued to love it. "Do you think they'll have the race next year?" joked Bill Rodgers after the 25th was in the record books.

Everyone knew the answer.

1978 2002

Boilermaker[SM]

15K ROAD RACE UTICA, NEW YORK

YEARS

1978-2002

Perennial Runners

The following twenty runners have run all twenty-five Utica Boilermaker Road Races.

Name: Bob Bluey

Age: 52

Residence: Yorkville, N.Y.

Best time: 1:03:25

2002 time: 1:19:32

Occupation: Program manager, Utica Corporation.

Family: Wife Linda, sons Rob and Matt.

Closest miss: Broke big toe in 1984 and was on crutches for the two weeks before the race. Ran despite doctor's recommendation not to.

When and why he began running: "In 1974. I ran the New York Mills Turkey Trot, a 1-mile race, and was in poor condition. I decided to get into shape with the encouragement of Joe Ficarro."

Running superstitions: None. "Runners are not superstitious. They are realists."

Favorite races: Millers Mills Sundae Run is a close second to the Boilermaker.

Favorite running shoes: Nike Air. "As comfortable as it gets."

Running partner: Joe Wilczynski for more than twenty years. "He's a big guy who blocks the wind for me."

Quote: "The race itself is just the best thing that Utica has today, and in the time I've lived in Utica it's probably the greatest event I've been involved with. It's Utica itself. It's the Boilermaker. It typifies the whole community."

Bob Bluey

Sheila Burth

Gordon Custodero

Name: Sheila Burth

Age: 38

Residence: New Hartford, N.Y.

Best time: 1:02:25

2002 time: 1:24:15

Occupation: Physical therapist.

Family: Daughter Cassie.

Closest miss: In 1996 she tore a calf muscle while teaching aerobics during Memorial Day weekend.

When and why she began running: "At age thirteen. I began to run track and it was something my mother and I could do together."

Running superstitions: Saucony running shoes and orthotics from Dr. Mark Schug.

Favorite races: None.

Favorite running shoes: Saucony.

Running partner: "I use the time to run to de-stress. My favorite companion is myself."

Quote: "I love to run and have been able to run for twenty-five years. My family runs the Boilermaker and it's become like Christmas or Easter—a time to celebrate with family and friends. It is a celebration of my ability to keep running a family."

Name: Gordon "Butch" Custodero

Age: 55

Residence: New Hartford, N.Y.

Best time: 1:09:00

2002 time: 1:27:22

Occupation: Retired teacher.

Family: Wife Kay, daughters Marie, Linda and Ann.

Closest miss: "My leg was crushed when I was hit by a car two days after the Boilermaker one year."

When and why he began running: "I started running in college [1965] to stay in shape. I ran in Converse All-Stars."

Running superstitions: None.

Favorite races: None.

Favorite running shoes: Saucony.

Running partner: Usually runs alone.

Quote: "Once I started, it was hard to stop. The Boilermaker motivates me to stay in shape and run another Boilermaker. The Boilermaker is important to me because I've run with each of my children, my wife, nieces and friends. It has become a tradition that brings our family and friends together — and it's a great excuse for a party."

Name: Wayne Decker
Age: 66
Residence: Whitesboro, N.Y.
Best time: 1:02:10
2002 time: 1:15:15
Occupation: Retired.
Family: Wife Gail, daughter Jeanine, sons Randy and David.
Closest miss: None.
When and why he began running: "In 1975. I have always been active in sports either participating or officiating. Looking for something different, a friend suggested running, and I've been running ever since."
Running superstitions: None.
Favorite races: Falling Leaves, Summer Sizzle, Heart Run.
Favorite running shoes: New Balance.
Running partners: Dan Cohen, Tom Hovey and Howard Rubin.
Quote: "The Boilermaker weekend is a great event I look forward to every year. It has become an important part of my running career. It means completing a personal goal that I have set for myself. I am proud to be a part of a group of runners who are dedicated to the race and the community. It is one of the top races in the country and benefits our local economy.

"I just like the exercise. I train all year round and I try to keep my body in excellent condition. Also, the competition, that's another thing I like. All year round I'm active. I cross-country ski and play basketball. The main thing is exercise itself."

Name: Daniel DeFrees
Age: 47
Residence: Rochester, N.H. (originally from Chittenango, N.Y.)
Best time: 57:20
2002 time: 1:13:55
Occupation: Shoe store manager.
Family: Wife Lori, twin daughters Kelley and Molley, son Jacob.
Closest miss: None.
When and why he began running: "In 1977 to lose weight and get in shape to play basketball."
Running superstitions: None.
Favorite races: Mount Washington Road Race and Yellow Brick Road Run.
Favorite running shoes: Like them all.
Running partner: In Central New York, Ed MacDonald and David Hatch. In New Hampshire, Mike Andrews, John Dinella and Don Yeaton.
Quote: "I run the Boilermaker every year because I can. It's where it all started. It gives my running a focal point and purpose through the year. It was the first race of any kind I ever ran. It started what has been a 25-year love affair with the sport. I became involved in the athletic-shoe business through running and it has been a big part of my personal and professional life. I can't imagine not running, or not running the Boilermaker.

"Another thing about the Boilermaker: I think there is no community that gets behind a race like Utica. I don't think there is anything like it anywhere. It's not just the Boilermaker, either. It's the Falling Leaves and the Heart Run, too."

Wayne Decker

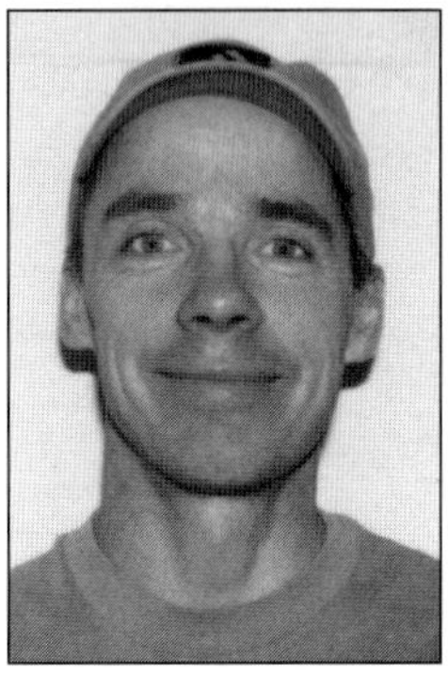

Daniel DeFrees

Lawrence P. DiCesare

Fred Gachowski

Name: Lawrence P. DiCesare

Age: 47

Residence: Sauquoit, N.Y.

Best time: 1:04:00 plus

2002 time: 1:02:00

Occupation: Administrator, Eden Park Health Care Center.

Family: Wife Polly, daughter Krista and son Larry.

Closest miss: None.

When and why he began running: "In 1978, right before the first Boilermaker."

Running superstitions: "I listen to 1970s rock music before the race."

Other favorite races: None.

Favorite running shoes: None.

Running partner: Keith Heinrich in the past. People from the neighborhood, my son. Harvey Cramer and Bobby Russo.

Quote: "I think most about where I have come from and where I am now in life. As an example, I ran my first Boilermaker in 1978 as a lark, by myself, in ordinary sneakers not knowing much about running.

"In 2002, I'll run my 25th Boilermaker with my nineteen-year-old daughter and chasing my seventeen-year-old son—a member of Sauquoit Valley's 2001 New York State champion cross-country team—as my wife, family and friends cheer us on. Life doesn't get much better than that."

Name: Fred Gachowski

Age: 63

Residence: New Hartford, N.Y.

Best time: Low 60s

2002 time: 1:30:11

Occupation: Retired from Niagara Mohawk.

Family: Daughters Michele, Laureen and Lynne.

Closest miss: None.

When and why he began running: "I read Kenneth Cooper's book *Aerobics* in 1967."

Running superstitions: None.

Favorite races: Boston Marathon, Waldo Canyon and Garden of the Gods 10K (both in Colorado) and Lilac Bloomsday.

Favorite running shoes: Started in New Balance and still running in New Balance.

Running partner: "I run alone and I run trails."

Quote: "It has gotten to be a big thing. I'd always been a casual runner and there was a friend at work who was a friend of Earle Reed's, so I ran. It gave me something to train for every year. I was never a competitive runner. It's the one thing that's kept me running. The whole experience is positive. There is nothing negative about the Boilermaker. It's all positive."

William Gazitano

Donald Harvey

Name: William Gazitano
Age: 51
Residence: Utica, N.Y.
Best time: 1:05:56
2002 time: 2:04:04
Occupation: Social worker.
Family: Stepson Shawn Merritt.
Closest miss: 1980, started the race late.
When and why he began running: "I ran high school track, was a fair-weather runner in college and beyond. Joined a fitness club at the Rome Family Y in 1978, ran first race in April 1978 and then ran the first Boilermaker. The incentive was to stay in shape."
Running superstitions: Fear of getting completely out of shape.
Favorite races: Falling Leaves, Thanksgiving Day Run.
Favorite running shoes: New Balance.
Running partner: None, but occasionally Utica Road Runners and co-workers at the Heart Run.
Quote: "I run to stay in shape, and do other exercises. The Boilermaker is a great showing of community spirit. It shows that a small city like Utica can rally and have the support of thousands of volunteers to make the race a great success, and an event that people from around the world look forward to participating in. Yet it still is a local phenomenon as well. Around here, the quality of people is one of the greatest resources.

"It is a symbol of diversity in a small, traditional city, reflecting how we have welcomed people from other countries to our area, in the past and more recently through the Refugee Center. The winners might have names unfamiliar to us, but we can be grateful for their presence here."

Name: Donald Harvey
Age: 58
Residence: Utica, N.Y.
Best time: 1:06:03
2002 time: 1:20:57
Occupation: Retired program manager, Air Force Research Laboratory, Griffiss Business Park.
Family: Wife Marlene, sons David and Tyler, daughters Brenda and Melissa.
Closest miss: Several. Burned foot the week before one race. Ran with a bandage.
When and why he began running: "In the late 1960s for exercise. As the distance grew I began to enjoy a runner's high. It's a natural drug effect and it's free—you pay in sweat."
Running superstitions: "Never quit on a hill."
Favorite races: None right now.
Favorite running shoes: New Balance: "Second best isn't close."
Running partner: None right now.
Quote: "It's a great crowd and community event and I love the hoopla, especially the YMCA song coming down onto Court Street. The run forces me to condition more than I would otherwise by running more miles. I enjoy seeing some of my friends after the race, although many no longer run it. Running as an exercise is excellent and if there is a fountain of youth and physical well-being, it is exercise. This country needs to get off its collective rear end and move. I have had serious health problems [back surgery, knee surgery, rheumatoid arthritis] and exercise is great medicine."

Paul Huening

Don Keinz

Name: Paul Huening

Age: 55

Residence: Utica, N.Y.

Best time: 1:07:49

2002 time: 1:48:59

Occupation: Manager, Mitten Mfg., Syracuse, N.Y.

Family: Wife Penny, daughter Jana, sons Paul and Matt.

Closest miss: "The first Boilermaker. We moved into our home that same weekend."

When and why he began running: About four months before the first Boilermaker. "A group of us who worked at Remington Arms with Larry Frederick were inspired and coached by him to run that first race."

Running superstitions: None.

Favorite races: The old Adam Helmer Marathon.

Favorite running shoes: Nike.

Running partner: Early years, Bob Hargrove. Currently, occasionally with son Matt, who has run the last seven Boilermakers.

Quote: "I really can't imagine not running a Boilermaker. From the beginning it has been an annual family event that we have all enjoyed. The high quality of the race and the support given by the spectators, volunteers and the community has made it the premier event for the greater Utica area. I looked forward to the 25th with as much anticipation and excitement as I have for all the others."

Name: Don Keinz

Age: 48

Residence: Wrentham, Mass. (originally from New Hartford, N.Y.)

Best time: 53:48

2002 time: 1:03:22

Occupation: Owner of Acadia Consulting Group, a marketing/consulting firm in Providence, R.I.

Family: Wife Anne, daughter Kristin.

Closest miss: "Five years ago, after a knee operation. I began training and reinjured it, then didn't fill out an application. Race director Earle Reed and assistant director Joe Kelly got me into the race late. I'll never forget those guys for that."

When and why he began running: Ran cross-country at New Hartford High School and at Hartwick College.

Running superstitions: "I always play Bruce Hornsby and The Range's 'It's A Long, Long Race' on the way driving over."

Favorite races: "This is truly my favorite."

Favorite running shoes: Adidas.

Running partners: Wife Anne

Quote: "For me, it's a connection to Central New York. That's the reason I come back, to reconnect with Upstate New York, which I absolutely love. We plan our vacation every year coming back for the Boilermaker. My daughter, Kristin, is going to run it for the first time. My wife, Anne, has run it five or six times."

Name: Connie LaSalle
Age: 66
Residence: Albany, N.Y. (originally from Whitesboro, N.Y.)
Best time: 1:16:00 plus
2002 time: 1:34:26
Occupation: Homemaker for forty years, also worked for Met Life.
Family: Sons Mark and Bob.
Closest miss: A pulled back muscle, but ran anyway.
When and why she began running: "In 1974 because my two sons, Bob and Mark, were running cross-country in school, at Oriskany."
Running superstitions: None.
Favorite races: Half-marathon in Kingston, Ontario and Lake Placid Half Marathon.
Favorite running shoes: Saucony Jazz Grid.
Running partner: Dolores Quinn.
Why she runs the Boilermaker: "It's a local race and I think as the years have gone by the excitement with the community participation keeps me coming back to do it. And I love the course. It's a great course."

Name: Robert Morris
Age: 65
Residence: New Hartford, N.Y.
Best time: 1:05:00
2002 time: 1:48:06
Occupation: Salesman.
Family: Wife Becky, sons Bob and David and daughter Cathy.
Closest miss: None.
When and why began running: In 1971 or 1972 for health conditioning.
Running superstitions: None.
Favorite races: "I like them all if I can finish them."
Favorite running shoes: None. "I've tried them all."
Running partner: Wife Becky, Bob Ingalls, Eddie Williams and Tom Hovey.
Quote: "It's the highlight of the year. It gives us something to plan for every year. [Becky is a top Boilermaker masters runner.] I used to run every weekend. Now we run the Boilermaker. It's a great bunch of people to associate with."

Connie LaSalle

Robert Morris

Ed Newman

Name: Ed Newman

Age: 40

Residence: Ontario, N.Y. (originally from New York Mills, N.Y.)

Best time: Low 50s

2002 time: 1:09:01

Occupation: Insurance special claims representative.

Family: Wife Susan, son Brett, daughters Elizabeth and McKenzie.

Closest miss: "The committee didn't get my registration one year. Tony Parretta gave up his number to me and the committee re-registered me."

When and why he started running: "My parents didn't want me to play football and my seventh-grade math teacher, Jim Dever, wanted to start a junior high cross-country team and he asked me to run. He was a great role model who taught us about discipline, respect, being healthy and about running."

Running superstitions: "Don't forget your running shoes when you live out of town."

Favorite races: Cazenovia V8 race.

Favorite running shoes: Saucony or New Balance.

Running partner: "In school, my friend Rob Green. I start each race with my brother Jim when he runs."

Quote: "Of course, one has to enjoy it to keep running for all these years. The race weekend is special because it is like a family reunion as my brothers and sisters come in from three different states.

"My dad always drives us to the starting line the morning of the race and then heads out to one of his cheering sites along the route. I'll see aunts and uncles and a couple of my elementary school teachers on the golf course or Parkway. My mother will be around UC with my wife and kids and all along the route are people I don't know who seem to be cheering each runner on.

"The party after the race at the brewery is like no other that I have ever seen. Thinking about the jet flyover last year still gives me chills.

"After the race, we head back to Mom and Dad's for a swim and plenty of good food.

"Why run it every year? I guess I hadn't thought about it much. It's just what we do the second Sunday of July every year."

Name: Paul Ohlbaum
Age: 67
Residence: New Hartford, N.Y.
Best time: 1:02:10
2002 time: 1:29:46
Occupation: Retired optometrist.
Family: Wife Billie, daughter Diana, son Steve.
Closest miss: "Never came close. It's on my personal calendar a year ahead."
When and why he began running: "I read Ken Cooper's *Aerobics* in 1968."
Running superstitions: "None, but I always wear a singlet or T-shirt with 'Utica' on it."
Favorite races: Falling Leaves (He's run every one of them, too.) and the Utica Parkway Development Runs—"The best family event in the area and a big reason for the success of the Boilermaker and Falling Leaves."
Favorite running shoes: Brooks and Mizuno.
Running partners: Formerly Tom Hovey, Sam Gratch, Art Golden, Earle Reed and Dave Pearce, then Al Pylman, Nancy Castellano, Chuck Silverman, Mark Blaker, Tony Iannone, now son Steve and daughter-in-law Barbara.
Quote: "Why run the Boilermaker every year? 'Cause it's there. I don't know. I feel I have to. My wife says I still enjoy the competition and I like the social part of it. And as long as there is someone behind me, I feel good."

Name: Thomas Pasek
Age: 60
Residence: Deerfield, N.Y.
Best time: Can't recall
2002 time: 1:54:30
Occupation: Purchasing/sales manager for Central Association for Blind and Visually Impaired.
Family: Wife Martha, sons Andy, Matt and Dan, daughter Christine.
Closest miss: None.
When and why he began running: "I was encouraged by Paul Ohlbaum. He talked me into that first race."
Running superstitions: None.
Other favorite races: Pitt Run in Oneonta.
Favorite running shoes: None.
Running partners: None.
Quote: "I don't run for the time. I run for the experience. My sons and wife and daughter all have run. It's a family thing. If you are going to live here, you have to participate in these things and enjoy the flavor of the area, and this is one great flavor to enjoy. It is a great family event."

Paul Ohlbaum

Thomas Pasek

James Tierney

Ken Virtuoso

Name: James Tierney

Age: 74

Residence: Saratoga, N.Y. (originally from Syracuse, N.Y.)

Best time: 1:21:00

2002 time: 1:51:18

Occupation: Health care.

Family: Wife Dolores.

Closest miss: 1980, back pain.

When and why he began running: "In 1952, for enjoyment."

Running superstitions: None.

Favorite races: Key Run, FireCracker, Stockadathon and Chopperthon 10K.

Favorite running shoes: Saucony Grid.

Running partners: None.

Quote: "The Boilermaker is habit-forming—the crowd involvement and support. It's the greatest 15K in the USA."

Name: Ken Virtuoso

Age: 53

Residence: Rome, N.Y.

Best time: 59:27

2002 time: 1:16:52

Occupation: Quality assurance specialist, Central New York Developmental Disabilities Services Offices.

Family: Wife Andrea, daughter Erica.

Closest miss: In 1996 because of a business trip.

When and why he began running: "To get in shape for playing football in college."

Running superstitions: "A red headband during the Boilermaker."

Favorite races: The Marine Corps Marathon, Ottawa Marathon.

Favorite running shoes: Asics.

Running partner: "I'll run with anyone."

Quote: "One of the reasons I run is my personal evolution. I've been running almost all my life. It helps define who I am."

Name: Richard Watkajtys
Age: 54
Residence: New Hartford, N.Y.
Best time: 1:01:32, 1983
2002 time: 1:28:25
Occupation: Workers Compensation Supervisor at Utica National Insurance.
Family: Wife Donna, sons Matthew and Nathan.
Closest miss: "I broke a toe and didn't run a step for six weeks, right up till race time."
When and why he began running: "My wife gave me Jim Fixx's *The Complete Book of Running* and the running bug hit hard."
Running superstitions: "All my lucky stuff has worn out over 25 years."
Favorite races: New York City, Boston, Marine Corps, San Francisco, Ottawa, Buffalo Skylon Marathons and especially the Dublin City Marathon.
Favorite running shoes: Asics.
Running partner: Jacques, his Irish setter: "We do 3 miles every morning and he tends to set the pace. Honest."
Quote: "The race means a lot of different things. Although you are the one running, it tends to be a family affair. My wife, dad and late mom have been spectators on many if not all occasions, and now my children, as well. Good friends either run or watch the race and Boilermaker weekend is a good time to get together and reminisce about the past races and good old times we had growing up.

"Jim Morgan [the late Family Court judge] was a good friend who ran many of the races and we have a brick across from each other in Boilermaker Park. I plan to wear the 'Jim Morgan' singlet again in his memory for this 25th event and will wear 'Stars & Stripes' shorts in the aftermath of 9/11."

Name: Joe Wilczynski
Age: 43
Residence: Marcy, N.Y.
Best time: 1:03:50
2002 time: 1:21:51
Occupation: Field representative, Dormitory Authority, State of New York.
Family: Wife Susanne, daughter Erica.
Closest miss: 1993, after a heel operation.
When and why he began running: "In 1976 for health reasons."
Running superstitions: None.
Favorite races: Heart Run, Hall of Fame Run, Run for the Rescue.
Favorite running shoes: New Balance 991.
Running partner: Robert Bluey for 24 years.
Quote: " I believe the Boilermaker is one of the greatest sporting events in our area and to watch this race grow throughout the 25 years of my involvement is a thrill. I look forward to participating every year. It means participating in the best 15K road race in the country. I have run the New York City Marathon, Philadelphia Marathon and many road races all over, but the fans that support us along the course, in my opinion, are the best in the country."

Richard Watkajtys

Joe Wilczynski

1978-2002

Boilermaker Statistics

Inaugurated in 1978

Course recertified by TAC 1985
(Starting line pushed back 399 feet to match new requirements.)

New course, certified 1997
(Adjustment in course on Genesee Street after the starting line moved up 360 yards to accommodate additional runners.)

All-time Course Records

Men .... Joseph Kimani, Kenya, 42:54, 1997
Women .... Catherine Ndereba, Kenya, 48:06, 2001
Men's Masters .... Andrew Masai, Kenya, 44:56, 2000
Women's Masters .... Elena Fidatov, Romania, 52:01, 2002
Wheelchair Men .... Saul Mendoza, USA, 32:40, 2000
Wheelchair Women .... Laurie Stephens, USA, 46:26, 2000

Race Records *(including old course, before 1997)*

Men .... Joseph Kimani, Kenya, 42:40, 1996
Women .... Catherine Ndereba, Kenya, 48:06, 2001
Men's Masters .... Andrew Masai, Kenya, 44:56, 2000
Women's Masters .... Elena Fidatov, Romania, 52:01, 2002
Wheelchair Men .... Saul Mendoza, USA, 32:40, 2000
Wheelchair Women .... Rose Winand, USA, 46:08, 1996

1978

Men .... Ric Rojas, USA, 45:38
Women .... Kathy Mills, USA, 54:26
Men's Masters .... Kenneth Mueller, USA, 50:39
Women's Masters .... Pat Bessell, USA, 1:05:04

1979

Men .... Tom Carter, USA, 47:15
Women .... Cindy Girard, USA, 57:30
Men's Masters .... Brian Harris, USA, 50:58
Women's Masters .... Barbara Backer, USA, 1:10:17

1980

Men .... Peter Pfitzinger, USA, 45:16
Women .... Nancy Mieszczak, USA, 55:02
Men's Masters .... Calvin Loomis, USA, 52:05
Women's Masters .... Becky Morris, USA, 1:09:27
Wheelchair Men .... Marty Ball, USA, 53:30 (approx.)

1981

Men .... Terry Baker, USA, 44:48
Women .... Mary Rybinski, USA, 54:49
Men's Masters .... Ralph Zimmerman, USA, 48:51
Women's Masters .... Pat Bessell, USA, 1:00:46
Wheelchair Men .... Colin Dye, USA, 1:05:29

1982

Men .... James O'Connell, USA, 44:58
Women .... Laura DeWald, USA, 54:41
Men's Masters .... Kirk Randall, USA, 49:44
Women's Masters .... Setsu Rosen, USA, 1:07:50
Wheelchair Men .... Marty Ball, USA, Time not available

1983

Men .... Bill Rodgers, USA, 44:38
Women .... Ena Guevara-Mora, USA, 53:22
Men's Masters .... Ernest Dumas, USA, 50:10
Women's Masters .... Betsy O'Neill, USA, 1:04:58
Wheelchair Men .... Marty Ball, USA, 48:06

1984

Men .... Geoff Smith, Great Britain, 44:21
Women .... Ena Guevara-Mora, USA, 52:36
Men's Masters .... Kenny Inglis, Canada, 48:12
Women's Masters .... Cindy Dalrymple, USA, 55:25
Wheelchair Men .... Not Available

1985

Men .... Jerry Kiernan, Ireland, 44:42
Women .... Judi St. Hilaire, USA, 50:35
Men's Masters .... Ralph Zimmerman, USA, 51:05
Women's Masters .... Cindy Dalrymple, USA, 59:02
Wheelchair Men .... Jeff Koch, USA, 46:53

1986

Men .... Joseph Kipsang, Kenya, 44:07
Women .... Lisa Welch, USA, 50:19
Men's Masters .... Graham Tattersall, New Zealand, 48:50
Women's Masters .... Diane Palmason, Canada, 1:01:33
Wheelchair Men .... Bill McGovern, USA, 49:25

1987

Men .... Mark Roberts, Great Britain, 45:10
Women .... Becky Kirsininkas, USA, 54:10
Men's Masters .... Atlaw Beligne, USA, 50:26
Women's Masters .... Bobbi Rothman, USA, 57:17
Wheelchair Men .... Tom Nowhitney, USA, 59:00

1988
Men .... Joseph Kipsang, Kenya, 44:55
Women .... Ria Van Landeghem, Belgium, 52:45
Men's Masters .... Bob Shlau, USA, 48:32
Women's Masters .... Barb Filutze, USA, 57:05
Wheelchair Men .... Bill McGovern, USA, 53:34

1989
Men .... Jon Sinclair, USA, 44:06
Women .... Michelle Bush-Cuke, USA, 52:35
Men's Masters .... Wilson Waigwa, Kenya, 46:09
Women's Masters .... Ngaire Drake, New Zealand, 55:05
Wheelchair Men .... Tom Nowhitney, USA, 1:03:16

1990
Men .... Delmir Dos Santos, Brazil, 44:01
Women .... Maria Trujillo, Mexico, 51:39
Men's Masters .... John Campbell, New Zealand, 45:10
Women's Masters .... Nancy Grayson, USA, 55:08
Wheelchair Men .... Bill McGovern, USA, 48:50

1991
Men .... Ed Eyestone, USA, 44:10
Women .... Jill Hunter, Great Britain, 48:19
Men's Masters .... Manuel Vera, Mexico, 45:57
Women's Masters .... Nancy Grayson, USA, 55:15
Wheelchair Men .... Colin Dye, USA, 44:04
Wheelchair Women .... Connie Head, USA, 1:02:39

1992
Men .... Sammy Lelei, Kenya, 43:39
Women .... Madina Biktagirova, Russia, 50:22
Men's Masters .... Pierre Levisse, France, 45:08
Women's Masters .... Nancy Grayson, USA, 54:58
Wheelchair Men .... Marty Ball, USA, 45:06
Wheelchair Women .... Connie Head, USA, 54:49

1993
Men .... Thomas Osano, Kenya, 43:39
Women .... Gitte Karlshoj, Denmark, 51:07
Men's Masters .... Nick Rose, Great Britain, 46:00
Women's Masters .... Carol McLatchie, USA, 54:56
Wheelchair Men .... Chris Waddell, USA, 41:41
Wheelchair Women .... Connie Head, USA, 57:08

1994
Men .... Benson Masya, Kenya, 42:57
Women .... Delillah Asiago, Kenya, 50:24
Men's Masters .... Martin Mondragon, Mexico, 45:28
Women's Masters .... Diane Legare, Canada, 55:38
Wheelchair Men .... Chris Waddell, USA, 40:17
Wheelchair Women .... Harrilyn Beehner, USA, 1:16:25

1995
Men .... Lazarus Nyakeraka, Kenya, 43:09
Women .... Rosali Machado, Brazil, 49:42
Men's Masters .... Martin Mondragon, Mexico, 45:26
Women's Masters .... Lorraine Moller, New Zealand, 53:16
Wheelchair Men .... John Rodolph, USA, 42:56
Wheelchair Women .... Connie Head, USA, 1:12:30

1996
Men .... Joseph Kimani, Kenya, 42:40
Women .... Catherine Ndereba, Kenya, 48:55
Men's Masters .... Karel Jircik, Canada, 47:29
Women's Masters .... Tatyana Pozdnyakova, Ukraine, 52:03
Wheelchair Men .... Tony M. Nogueira, USA, 36:15
Wheelchair Women .... Rose Winand, USA, 46:08

1997
(First year of course adjustment, start near Beechgrove Place and four turns added off Parkway, Genesee, Shepherd Place, Sunset to Burrstone Road.)
Men .... Joseph Kimani, Kenya, 42:54
Women .... Lornah Kiplagat, Kenya, 49:58
Men's Masters .... Martin Mondragon, Mexico, 46:47
Women's Masters .... Joan Benoit Samuelson, USA, 53:23
Wheelchair Men .... Saul Mendoza, USA, 34:05
Wheelchair Women .... Jessica Galli, USA, 52:18

1998
Men .... Khalid Khannouchi, Morocco, 42:57
Women .... Lornah Kiplagat, Kenya, 50:06
Men's Masters .... Peter Koech, Kenya, 47:16
Women's Masters .... Jane Welzel, USA, 53:21
Wheelchair Men .... Tony M. Nogueira, USA, 36:41
Wheelchair Women .... Jessica Galli, USA, 52:06

1999
Men .... John Korir, Kenya, 43:00
Women .... Catherine Ndereba, Kenya, 48:52
Men's Masters .... John Tuttle, USA, 46:17
Women's Masters .... Diane Legare, Canada, 55:48
Wheelchair Men .... Krige Schabort, USA, 33:35
Wheelchair Women .... Laurie Stephens, USA 46:57

2000
Men .... Reuben Cheruiyot, Kenya, 43:07
Women .... Catherine Ndereba, Kenya, 48:47
Men's Masters .... Andrew Masai, Kenya, 44:56
Women's Masters .... Marina Belyaeva, Russia, 53:47
Wheelchair Men .... Saul Mendoza, USA, 32:40
Wheelchair Women .... Laurie Stephens, USA, 46:26

2001
Men .... John Korir, Kenya, 42:57
Women .... Catherine Ndereba, Kenya, 48:06
Men's Masters .... Andrew Masai, Kenya, 45:13
Women's Masters .... Elena Fidatov, Romania, 53:18
Wheelchair Men .... Saul Mendoza, USA, 33:30
Wheelchair Women .... Jessica Galli, USA, 47:20

2002
Men .... Paul Kosgei, Kenya, 43:22
Women .... Constantina Dita, Romania, 48:29
Men's Masters .... Andrew Masai, Kenya, 46:25
Women's Masters .... Elena Fidatov, Romania, 52:01
Wheelchair Men .... Kamel B. Ayari, USA, 36:53
Wheelchair Women .... April Coughlin, USA, 50:53